Rediscovering Friendship

Elisabeth Moltmann-Wendel

scm press

Translated by John Bowden from the German
*Wache auf, meine Freundin. Die Wiederkehr der
Gottesfreundschaft,* published 2000 by
Kreuz Verlag, GmbH & Co. KG Stuttgart.

0 334 02818 3

This edition first published 2000 by
SCM Press
9–17 St Albans Place London N1 0NX

SCM Press is a division of
SCM-Canterbury Press Ltd

Typeset by Regent Typesetting, London
Printed in Great Britain by
Biddles Ltd, Guildford and King's Lynn

For my grand-daughter Eliza

Contents

Introduction

To illustrate the start of women's culture at the beginning of the previous century, Virginia Woolf devised a fictitious novel by a fictitious author. Its subject was the life of two women, and she noted her amazement as follows:

> 'Chloe liked Olivia,' I read. And then it struck me how immense a change was there. Chloe liked Olivia perhaps for the first time in literature . . . And I tried to remember any case in the course of my reading where two women are represented as friends . . . But almost without exception they are shown in their relation to men . . . And how small a part of a woman's life is that; and how little a man knows even of that when he observes it through the black or rosy spectacles which he puts upon his nose.

So here Virginia Woolf discovered not just friendship between women as it always had been, but above all friendship as a private and personal relationship. She discovered a new, open, social relationship between women which rested on the fact that women use 'pens and brushes and business and politics' and thus give an indication of the 'extremely complex force of femininity'. As she saw it, 'Women have sat indoors all those millions of years, so that for this time the very walls are permeated by their creative force . . . But this creative power differs greatly from the creative power of men.'[1] The pressure of dumbness, the accumulation of life which has not been spoken of, is broken out of and a new friendship between women becomes real. In it women also share new spheres like adventure, art and knowledge; it is also a path towards lesbian love.

Women are now becoming more conscious of what began in the 1920s. A new quality of friendship, of the kind that we encounter in the patterns described by Mary Hunt and Hildegund Keul, is emerging.

For a long time our pattern of friendship was governed by male friendship between equals who become more intimate in an intellectual dialogue about truth. This is an image which goes back to Aristotle. For Nietzsche, woman was still capable only of love and not of this kind of friendship, and in *Das Grosse Brockhaus*, the major German dictionary, as late as 1988, models of male friendship were still dominant. Here friendship is described as 'ritualized (like Greek friendship between youths and men), as institutionalized and under social protection (as in blood brotherhood), or as an alliance (as in the German associations)'. Only after that are the 'pair-group' and the looser types of friendship, like acquaintance, added.

However, above all after the French Revolution, when women made great efforts to find a place in public through their words and books and in the salon, a process began which produced impressive cultures of friendship from the 'avant-garde without hinterland' – a description given by Christa Wolf to the early friendships between women.[2] Thus in her salon in Berlin the Jewish woman Rachel Varnhagen demonstrated that friendship between women also indicates the equality of the sexes and thus is a prelude to a democracy. At the same time she called her relatives, her brothers and sisters-in-law, 'friends' and made it clear that friendship could infiltrate blood ties.[3] Friendship as a political fact and freedom from the constraints of the family are still important elements in understanding friendship between women.

Thus friendship between women introduces new emphases: in it public and private characters are combined. It flourishes in everyday life, awakens hitherto unknown energies, and creates freedom from family ties. It also brings openness to same-sex relationships between women, and to homosexual partnerships.

There is friendship as a political factor, friendship as freedom for other forms of life, friendship as earthing – as a source of the discovery of one's own personality and as a liberation from rigid forms of life. However, at present these are more wishful descriptions than realities. There are still the old models in our culture.

There is the niche of women's friendship in a culture dominated by men, in which all frustration is left behind and consolation is sought in the friend. The bosom friend is still a social and psychological necessity for women. On the other hand, the male friendship which is governed by self-interest, which hardly abandons its own self and knows virtually no intimacy, is still very much there. But alongside forms of friendship which are distorted because they are encapsulated, open forms of life are also developing which no longer confront the other or others in a way which ranges from the guarded to the hostile.

The great diversity of forms of friendship today is striking, and above all the quest for friendly self-descriptions. Thus often not only do parents put notices in the paper announcing the death of a son or daughter, but the same is done by groups of friends for one of their number. Yasmin, Nina and Nico want to show that they are just as affected as parents and family and to demonstrate this publicly.

According to a survey by the journal *Der Spiegel* (12 July 1999), young people spend as much as eighty-five per cent of their spare time with friends; and only thirteen per cent mention television as their main spare-time activity,

In my view, a cultural change is taking place in which family ties and family norms are fading into the background and being replaced by the most diverse kinds of groups of friends, on the same footing as the family or as a substitute for it.

The growing number of patchwork families is also leading to an increase in the number of relations between friends.

Does that mean that we are moving towards a friendly world? Or is the warmth of the group simply being sought to escape a cold and restricted world dominated by a competitive struggle?

Perhaps one consequence of looser notions of friendship is that the pattern of friendship also serves to suggest friendly relations between different groupings. Thus today people talk about friendly ecumenical relations, though such talk passes over the tricky questions of eucharist and ministry. 'Spiritual friendships at the parish level' are encouraged, characterized by both intimacy and distancing. An article about pastoral care says that the pastor need not necessarily be a preacher or helper, but it is essential for him or her to be 'friendly':

> Friendship is a better pattern of orientation for the pastor than preaching or ministry . . . In a gathering of a friendly kind there is room both for interest in fellow human beings and also a desire and the readiness to proclaim the gospel. The concepts of kerygma and diakonia tend to introduce constraints.[4]

Are we on the way towards a friendly culture which will see the replacement of domination, hierarchy and violence, along with a pattern of pastoral care which involves too much supervision and too little independence? Are we moving towards a culture characterized by an increase in friendly behaviour, in which the personal dignity of encounter is preserved, and yet commitment and empathy are not excluded? In recent decades attempts have been made in theological circles to use the term 'tenderness' in calling for new patterns of human behaviour and to replace the images of domination. God too was tender. Tenderness was one of the daughters of God, and 'unswervingly subversive'.[5] Later she was replaced above all by Lady Eros: erotic knowledge, eroticism as the food of life, became the new hierarchy-free slogans.⁶ But the solemnity which always goes with the two terms becomes wearisome. 'Friend', 'friendly' is less portentous and could replace its two predecessors. Still, it becomes clear from tenderness, eroticism and friendliness that various images are being sought in our culture to signal a new way of dealing with one another which will also enrich family relationships.

I would not want to make women's experience of friendship an absolute. However, I do see it as an important step forward from old patterns.

For me, God as friend is a healing image for our day. Anyone who is tired of the discussion about using the metaphors of father or mother for God, who misses a personal element in the images drawn from nature and the figure of Wisdom, can rediscover in friendship with God something of the breadth, closeness, goodness and companionship which people today so urgently need.

Klaus-Peter Jörns has shown that people today do not primarily ask about the gracious God but rather seek a partnership with God, God who stands beside them in the conflicts in their lives.⁷ Here the notion of friendship could be helpful and give new life to religious language.

However, since I have begun to speak of friendship with God, I keep getting asked whether the notion of friendship sufficiently enables us 'to perceive and reconcile the different dimensions of God and human beings and the abysses between them, and not to overlook this'. Such questions are usually asked by those who have been brought up on traditional theology, for whom the distance between God and human beings remains the one, steadfast and compelling topic of theology.

Others have problems about how God can be understood as friend in view of the disasters which are constantly visited upon the world. For them – as for many Christian men and women – God shares the responsibility for causing all the evil in this world.

And finally, there are those who experience friendship in such a private and intimate way that they find it almost impossible to see social and religious models in it.

Now 'God the friend' is an old biblical designation of God which keeps cropping up among Christians, but it no longer has a home in our theological thought-patterns and in our hierarchical bureaucratic churches. These are stamped by the distance between God and human beings. In feminist theology, too, 'God the friend' tends more to arouse the suspicion that here there is a transfer of male individualism.

However, God as friend is an image which regularly appears in the context of the search in which many people are engaged, for God as an ally who will support them in their problems. It is an image of the God-for-us and the God-with-us, the companion who can also become a sisterly companion, who helps us to cope with life in its complexity.

Those who have difficulties with such an image should take a look at the basic pattern of their own friendships. In friendship there is intimacy, trust and closeness. These are the basic presuppositions. A friend can also stand up for me, can make amends and can also be better than me. And like Job, I can also argue with my friends.

But in friendship there is also detachment, respect for the otherness of the other, the mystery of his or her strangeness. Only in this way can friendship be preserved from constant explosions. It is also possible to become alienated from one another and for a friendship to dissolve. Friendship can come to an end, yet time and again begin anew. A friendship can rest a while and then be revived.

I believe that we can rediscover all our experiences of friendship, including Eros and disillusionment, anger and reconciliation, strangeness and intimacy, in our experience with God, even if God as friend remains a mere metaphor, an attempt to say something about God. Here we can leave behind our childhood dreams or childhood dramas of the omnipotent Father who rules over all and also has all disasters in his hands. But sin is not denied in such a relationship with God. As is remarked by one of the women who will be portrayed later in this book, sin is separation from all others; it is not to use them or to be used by them. It is the refusal to recognize that we are dependent on all that lives. It is the refusal to be the eye and conscience of the cosmos. Sin means cutting oneself off from life, from God who – as Wisdom theology says – is a friend of life (Wisdom 11.26).

A theology which develops around friendship, which again experiences God as friend, is interested in salvation and well-being and justice for all. That is its starting point, its goal and its legitimation. Reflecting on God in terms of friendship can perhaps also enrich our own capacity for friendship. And there are some who think that they can experience God and the divine in friendship, God as a power in relationship. Friendship is a broad sphere which unites heaven and earth, which makes it possible to think of God and the divine in both immanent and transcendent terms.

However, we should beware of the old pirate cry, 'A friend of God and enemy to all the world!' That is still to be heard in theological circles dominated by a kind of theology of decision, between God and Satan. Here oppositions are pointed out which are incompatible with thinking in terms of friendship. Here is a repetition in a modern form of those crusades and wars of religion which once produced the fatal political theology advocated by Carl Schmitt and of use to the Nazis.[8]

Such either-or thinking as is still practised today is a fruit of that way of thinking in terms of friend and enemy which attempts to grasp reality in exclusive possibilities. However, it does not do justice to life. The psychotherapist Anne Wilson Schaef suggested replacing 'either-or' with 'both-and'; this makes communication easier and also enables us to give complex answers to complex problems.[9]

Finally, the American theologian Sallie McFague has pointed out to us that in Hebrew thought the opposite of friend is not enemy but stranger.[10] Friendship does not exclude strangers but includes them.

I want to describe notions of friendship with God first in the Bible and Christian tradition and then in contemporary theology. Here friendship with women, which will transform our traditional friendship, occupies a special place. However, I shall also often use the term 'friendship' for friendship exclusively with women. I shall also investigate models of friendship in christology, and their significance for the eucharist and the understanding of sin. Finally, Jesus' friend Mary Magdalene could provide an alternative image for the church to that of Peter, who once ran away. For me the notions of tenderness and Eros are also examples of the new quest for friendly social relations. Friendly behaviour in our bodies, which are still subject to domination and to our earth, which is still in leading reins, also make friendship concrete in our personal and public life. These contributions should be a stimulus to rediscovering friendship in many place and also learning friendship anew.[11]

In all this I do not want to suppress the family images which are to be found in the tradition, of being children of God and being sisters and brothers. They express a natural way of understanding relations with God and human beings which also signify independence. But with friendship we have a new expression of the precious, long-forgotten elements of freedom and responsibility which are helpful and life-transforming in a world that is changing at headlong speed. These elements can stand alongside the old images.

During the time when I have been occupied with the topic of friendship, many women have made important, critical and stimulating contributions. They have also referred me to books and translations. I could not include all the references in this volume, but they have steadily brought me one step closer to this complex topic. Here I want to thank most warmly all who have shared in my thinking. I would also like to thank

Hildegunde Wöller, my editor at Kreuz Verlag, for her skilful and friendly advice.

This unusual way of doing theology, and particularly feminist theology, has often made me lonely. So friendships, particularly over recent years, have been most important to me: the groups of Tübingen friends, the Zonta friendship, my old friends, and particularly my new ones. They have widened my perspectives, enriched me and given me a sense of being at home and belonging which I had long since lost. Once again my husband Jürgen Moltmann has supported me in the writing of this book with constant interest in the topics I have discussed. I am joined to him by a friendship of fifty years.

Elisabeth Moltmann-Wendel   Tübingen, October 1999

1

Traditions of Friendship with God

Friend and friendship are culturally conditioned notions in which there are a variety of emphases. Friendship with God is also an idea which can be found in Socrates, Plato, the Stoa, Hellenistic Judaism and the Mandaean literature. In Christianity we later have a diversity of influences.[1] Here I want to investigate the special biblical aspects of friendship with God and their influence on the history of theology.

The biblical basis

To begin with, four different strands in biblical thought can be brought out:

1. As elsewhere in the history of religion, 'friend of God' is a title which singles a person out. It still has the connotation of being elected, which for example the word *philos* has in Greek; here the friend is regarded as someone who is hallowed, initiated by God, and thus is elect. *Philos* (in the Greek translation of the Old Testament, the Septuagint) has this significance when Abraham is called 'friend' (Exodus 33.11; 41.8; James 2.23). Moses is also compared with a friend of God: 'The Lord spoke with Moses face to face, as a man speaks with his friend' (Exodus 33.11).

2. This election of individuals is later extended and democratized in wisdom theology. Anyone who acquires wisdom attains God's friendship (Wisdom 7.14). Wisdom can enter into

holy souls and make them friends of God and prophets (Wisdom 7.27). Wisdom's friends have truer joy, and inexhaustible riches come through the work of their hands (Wisdom 8.18). Wisdom can make someone a sister (Wisdom 8.18) and companion (Wisdom 8.9) and – as shrewdness – become a friend (Proverbs 7.4). The authoritarian notion of God is lost in wisdom theology and replaced with a fascinating play on images of friendship.

In wisdom theology God himself can also be a friend: God is a friend of life (Wisdom 11.26).

3. Exegetical studies, above all from the USA, show that the New Testament understanding of friendship is embedded in Graeco-Roman culture. Here I shall refer only to some aspects which are important for our present discussion.

In the New Testament Jesus calls people his friends: 'You are my friends if you do what I command you' (John 15.14); 'But I say to you, my friends, "Do not fear those . . . "' (Luke 12.4); 'Lazarus, our friend, is sleeping . . . .' (John 11.11).

Research shows that Jesus understood himself as Wisdom (Sophia, see p. 37 below). Thus these forms of address using the word 'friend' take on a special emphasis: they indicate closeness to God.

Judas, too, Jesus' closest companion, belongs among these friends. Jesus says to him, 'My friend, why have you come . . . ?' (Matthew 26.50).

Since women also belonged in the close fellowship of the disciples, we can imagine that they too were addressed as friends.

Jesus interprets his death as the death of a friend for his friends: 'Greater love has no one than this, that he lays down his life for his friends' (John 15.13). Here, too, the notion of election plays a role: 'You have not chosen me, but I have chosen you' (John 15.16). However, election is not to be understood in exclusive terms. To be elected means to be loved.

4. Outsiders call Jesus a 'friend of sinners and toll collectors'

(Matthew 11.19; Luke 7.34) and Jesus picks up this statement and identifies with it.

The friends in the fellowship of disciples as they are understood by the Gospel of John are joined in the Synoptic Gospels by another group of friends. Here the outcast are chosen as friends. Friends become those who by social criteria are unworthy. The understanding of friend takes on a new quality, indeed it changes.

The many examples of friends in Jesus' parables add yet more colour to friendship. Friendship is realized in sharing a meal. One invites friends to a meal. One is cheerful with friends and enjoys their company (Luke 15.11ff., 29; 14.10). The host in the parable of the royal marriage feast calls the person without a wedding garment 'friend' (Matthew 22.12; see also Luke 14.10). One is open to a friend, wants to enjoy things with him. Friendship is pleasurable, but it also involves obligations.

The charge that Jesus is a friend of sinners and toll collectors is also combined with the accusation that he eats with sinners (Luke 15.2) and is a glutton and drunkard (Luke 7.34; Matthew 11.19). In the Jesus movement, the most intimate fellowship, that of sharing a meal, has become a banquet of unusual friends, men and women, and these unusual friendships became a basic religious and social pattern of the Jesus movement.

The term 'friend' becomes an important designation of relationships in early Christianity, which is not based on any ties of blood or affinity. It indicates a community which represents a new society, a fellowship which not only integrates the outcasts but makes them the centre of the new society: it is a shared table at which they are guests of honour (Luke 14.12ff.). Here friendship is not just democratized but revolutionized. A provocative, unconventional culture of relationships begins with it.

As I pointed out earlier, a verse from the Letter of James plays an outsider's role in these notions of friendship: 'Do you not know that friendship with the world is enmity with God?' (4.4) Here we have an indication of that pattern of thinking in terms of friend and foe which later becomes so pernicious (see p. 7).

As I have already mentioned, Sallie McFague thinks that in the Bible the original basic opposite to friend is not enemy, but stranger. That presents a challenge to our thinking in terms of opposites and suggests a more process-orientated thinking. The stranger can become the guest and the friend. But in the New Testament the stranger is contrasted more with the citizen and the member of one's household (Ephesians 2.19).[2]

Bultmann points out the difficulty of the biblical concept of friendship, since Jesus does not call himself his disciples' friend, but only calls them his friends.[3] He therefore says that there is no indication of reciprocity on an equal footing. However, the use of 'friend' in wisdom theology tells against this, as does the example in the Gospel of Luke, where God is compared with a friend who is asked for a piece of bread at midnight (Luke 11.5). Here God is addressed as friend by human beings.

There are only two places in the New Testament where it is indicated that Christians also called one another friends, Acts 27.3 and III John 15. In Acts we are told that as a prisoner on the journey to Rome Paul is allowed to visit his 'friends' in Sidon. And in III John 'friends' are greeted by 'friends'.

Thus the word 'friend' did not become established in Christianity, perhaps because instead of friends – as the Johannine community understood the concept – Paul speaks of brothers (and sisters). Adolf von Harnack sees this as a 'more intimate and warmer notion'. However, he is also amazed at the loss of the term 'friend': 'One would have thought that the Christians too would have called one another "friends", but they hardly even begin to do so.'[4]

In my view Christians found it more natural to use family images for God and for relations among themselves. Like designations of God as friend, the bold concept of the *familia dei*, of those who came together in discipleship of their own free will, often breaking with their blood relations, got lost and emerged again in church history only sporadically. Today we are seeing a return of what was lost.

Later traces

Traces of friendship with God then occur above all in Clement of Alexandria and Origen. Martyrs in particular, but also apostles, saints, ascetics and church teachers are called friends of God in the subsequent period; so too sometimes are bishops, and time and again the term is used of Christians themselves. But opinions differed as to whether believers became friends of God at their creation or only at their redemption. For Hippolytus, humankind was the friend 'who has been created by the hands of God'. Tertullian held the other view, that human beings were innocent and friends of God only before the fall. Election to friendship or the acquisition of friendship similarly represented variant positions which also find no clear answers in the Bible.

Whereas Erik Peterson has made thorough investigations of the early church, we do not have sufficient knowledge of notions of friendship for the Middle Ages and modern times. Here I can give only a superficial survey:

In mediaeval mysticism, above all in the later period, notions of friendship with God also found a lively reception particularly among women.[5] Francis of Assisi was called *verus amicus et imitator Christi*, but in his sermons Bonaventura also repeatedly calls St Agnes *amica*, friend.

Meister Eckhart prefaces his collections of sermons with the sentence: 'I turn to you, brothers and sisters, who are God's dearest friends and at home with him.'[6]

References to the Johannine passages about friends recur time and again in Teresa of Avila. 'Christ,' she writes, ' is a good friend for us. We see him as a man, weak, suffering, as our companion. Once we have got used to that we can easily think of him . . . .'⁷ This friendship of God is then matched by friendship with one another in the wider fellowship.

In the mediaeval legends it is said of Mary Magdalene that Jesus 'kindled her wholly with his love' and accepted her 'as his special friend'.⁸

So in Christian history women, too, are declared to be friends of Jesus; this did not happen literally in the New Testament. Moreover women also took over the images of friendship.

In Paul Gerhardt's hymns, into which much of mediaeval mysticism has found its way, God and Jesus are directly addressed as friends: according to Bultmann, this does not happen in the biblical statements about friends.

The somewhat free English translations do not always indicate this, but it can be seen at the end of the famous 'O sacred head, sore wounded':

> That I may fight befriended,
> and see in my last strife
> to me thine arms extended
> upon the cross of life.

Thus mysticism makes good what Bultmann misses in the New Testament, the fact that there is also friendship with God from the human side.

Finally, two outsider groups have assumed the name of friends for their associations, thus developing the traces of what is begun in John. These are the 'Friends of God on the Lower Rhine', the fourteenth-century mystics, and the Quakers, the radical Protestants of the seventeenth century, who also called themselves 'The Society of Friends'.

At the time of the Reformation, Luther too took up the Johannine concept of friendship in order to interpret Galatians 3.28 (no longer male and female) 'in a way which is open to history'.⁹ In so doing he deliberately wanted to leave behind the traditional way of thinking in images drawn from the family. However, he did not draw the last conclusions for the structures of the church.

Even if at a later date friend all too often became 'soul friend' and thus became diverted into an intangible spiritual dimension, the notion and the use of the word 'friend' still always bore connotations of a social reality which also meant change.

The sparse use of images of friendship in church history can, however, make one mistrust a church culture which was more interested in obedient and dependent Christians, with imagery to match, than in independent 'friends' who stood on an equal footing. However, the continuation and development of these notions of the friend among free groups of Christians, in individual church teachers, in mysticism, and not least among women, provide a potential for the politics of church and society which has never been abandoned in Christian culture. Today the perspective is widening to take in relationships between women which are constantly suppressed yet always present, and mutual delight in God envisaged as a woman friend.

A woman writes: 'God is sometimes close to me, like a woman friend and close companion, but much more rarely like a male friend.' And: 'I sing of God as a woman friend because the femininity of God takes me directly into my relationship with God.'[10]

But what does friendship, and friendship with God, look like in contemporary theology? A long-forgotten topic seems to be being revived.

2

From Friendship with God to Friendship between Women

Jürgen Moltmann

Jürgen Moltmann, in 1975, was one of the first to take up again the concept of friendship from the tradition in order to use it to illuminate both interpersonal relationship and also relationships between God and human beings.[1] Here he was by no means concerned to retreat into individuality, but to make a contribution to the demolition of models of domination and the master-servant relationship in society and church: friendship is the 'soul of socialism'. Hegel called friendship the 'concrete concept of freedom'. But there is more to that in friendship: respect, concern, loyalty. If relationship with parents pales, friendship takes its place – a more mature human relationship; similarly, in the development of society, the master-servant relationship has to yield to a new relationship on an equal footing.

Starting from the friendship which Jesus practised in eating meals with toll collectors and sinners, Moltmann also sees the deeper sense of Jesus' relationship with people, a relationship which was long hidden under honorific titles. 'As prophet of the kingdom of God for the poor, Jesus becomes the friend of sinners and toll collectors. As high priest he sacrifices himself for the life and the salvation of others and completes his life by dying for his friends. As exalted Lord he liberates people from slavery and makes them friends of God.' Therefore a hierarchical official church should reflect again on the fact that it was once the community of the friends of sinners.

However, in order not to misunderstand friendship in exclusivist terms and to miss the significance of friendship in the New Testament, Moltmann proposes 'open friendship', a community which does not live in the inner circle of believers and pious but in open concern and public respect for others. Such open friendship then prepares the ground for a more friendly world.

Here friendship has become a key notion for a way of thinking in politics and theology which has both a horizontal and a vertical dimension. Others too discovered this key role in subsequent years.

Sallie McFague

Moltmann was followed in the 1980s by the American professor of theology, Sallie McFague, who wrote various studies which kept centring on the concept of friendship.

McFague is similarly fascinated by the social and religious dimension of friendship. She sees it as a contemporary model which can be used to speak convincingly of God and human relationships. However, it is a model which also needs corrections; she also uses other models alongside it.[2]

For her, too, the parent-child model which long was the centre of Christian talk of God is not exhaustive. She thinks that images of parents and children are no longer as central for our society as they were in former societies, and they can limit the notion of human life to ideals of procreation. Many people today, she argues, no longer intend to become parents and have children. Moreover she finds a hierarchical aspect in this model, rather than the aspects of reciprocity, maturity and responsibility which are contained in the image of friendship. Thirdly, our day needs notions of relations between diverse people, old and young, men and women, those of different races and religions. The image of friendship is appropriate for such collaboration and it can also express our relation to God.

Here friendship must be liberated from private and empathetic thought and become a kind of planetary thought. It must develop into friendship with the stranger and the unknown, whether these are nations or individuals: 'If people cannot become friends, they will not survive.'

As for Moltmann, so too for her the story of Jesus – the friend of toll collectors and sinners – his practice of sharing meals with the outcast is the starting point for such friendship. Here there has been a break with all hierarchy and social subordination, and this gives rise to equality and reciprocity. But McFague then asks urgently whether the authority of God is preserved in such an image of friendship. She shows that – in contrast to paternal authority – here a freely developing authority, including love and criticism, can unfold which is based on reciprocity and can produce new aspects of relationship which are not naturally given *a priori*. It is God who keeps fellowship with us and accompanies us along these ways.

She also asks how far in such an image God can still be seen as a healing, saving power; here she points to an image of God which no longer comprises solitude, omnipotence and isolation but also includes the partnership – and friendship – of men and women in their maturity and relationship to others. 'God's power is convincing, attractive, co-operative, and healing/ redemption is not a once-for-all act but a relationship to us and our world which grows as we respond to the longing of our friend to make us friends.' Here the traditional transcendence of God is transformed into an immanence, a life of God, which appeared in this world. God is part of us, as we share in the life of our friends.

However, McFague also refers to problems in such a notion of friendship, and does not want to see this 'experiment in thought' as an absolute. For her what are needed above all are also images which transcend the personal level and show the heights and depths of a God who is also cosmic. 'Ecstasy and terror cannot pass over into the images of God's parenthood or friendship – images of the ocean, heaven and earth can convey this better.'

McFague sets the notion of friendship in a contemporary theology in which the old images of God, consisting of omnipotence and domination, are replaced by images of the partnership of women and men with God and of the compassionate God. Given the diversity of aspects which she addresses, the one amazing thing is that the feminist aspect is touched on only as a hint: friendship, she says, is perhaps particularly relevant among women and in relation to men. However, she continues, friendship is also important for all men and women and for the whole of humankind.[3] She has not yet developed a special kind of friendship among women or the model of God as a woman friend.

Carter Heyward

In the same year, 1982, a book appeared in the USA which is still influential in feminist theology, *The Redemption of God. A Theology of Mutual Relation*. The author, Carter Heyward, introduced herself as a feminist, Christian and lesbian theologian and teacher whose deepest sources were human love and friendship.[4]

Friendship and friends are notions which permeate her theology and provide her basic pattern. Here she does not take up theological images, but sketches out a completely new structure of theological connections in which theology becomes politically significant and politics becomes theologically significant. Her aim is a world in which all men and women of the people of God are enabled by one another and by the God who works through all of us to live with dignity and sufficient nourishment, a world which will be both more human and also more divine. So friendship is a notion which belongs in both spheres.

First of all Heyward sets the notion of friendship alongside the relationship to God and in so doing protests against a distanced God who is separated from human beings, of the kind that keeps cropping up in theology. She also contrasts it with a solitary, Gnostic deity who has no friends. God is a friend, but this title does not exclude other titles. For her God is also what we can think of as mother or father, sister or beloved, friend or brother. These images express the notion of the constancy with which God builds bridges between us. In a phrase which has become classic, she says that God is 'the power in relationship'. And this relationship exists between plants and dogs and whales and mountains and towns and stars. Divine being drives us, longs for us, moves in us and through us and with us, in our recognizing ourselves as human beings and learning to love. We are basically in relationships and are not alone.

The God with this diversity of names, which Heyward keeps repeating, is the abundant and helpful God, our friend and brother who compels us to take up our bed and walk, to whom we can pray. He is the God whom we can affirm, the God of relationship and friendship, the God of justice for the poor, of justice for women, the God of justice for the outcast and 'the others' and the God of sexuality. This God is both Yahweh, the friend of humankind, and is as truly Goddess as she is God.

The notion of friendship now gives the intrinsically pale concept of relationship which stamps Heyward's theology warmth and movement. Friendship shows that relationship is mutual, and the joy of friendship can arise only in this way.

Such mutuality also occurs in the figure and story of Jesus. Jesus is God's child who grows in relationship to God and becomes God's friend in a voluntary and mutual relationship. The notions of 'father' and 'mother' indicate growth. 'Friend' denotes the successful mutual relationship which for Heyward can also be thought of the other way round: God as the child of Jesus.

Friendship also denotes the relationship of Jesus to those

around him, 'Jesus and his friends'. They are the bearers of the message of God; they change the world, and the Christian tradition is concentrated in them. But what Heyward fails to find in the Gospels are above all descriptions of the mutuality of the friendships of Jesus, especially in the passion narratives. She believes that the authors of the Gospels missed the core of the passion of Jesus, its roots in relationship. At this point, however, we need to ask whether mutuality and friendship are sufficient concepts to enable us to grasp fully the story of Jesus in its relationship to God and human beings. Heyward's interpretation of the Gethsemane scene points to a degree of violence which – as in other feminist sketches – bursts out at this point. Heyward interprets the cry 'My God, why have you forsaken me?' as an angry cry on the part of Jesus which had a particular focus: it expresses the lack of relationship, the broken relationship, the violated relationship, the destruction of God in the world. This Jesus who is in control of himself to the end thus loses some creatureliness, loneliness and humanity: all these are sacrificed to the mutuality that is sought. The limits of such mutuality seem to me to lie here.

Now it becomes important for Heyward not to see the resurrection of Jesus as an event in his life but as an event in the life of his friends. The death of Jesus helped his friends to refuse to give up the intimacy and immediacy of God. Jesus' image is the image of a friend, a human being whose friends, men and women, began to claim their own power. However, Jesus is not their head, without whom they could do nothing.

The social background to this passionate emphasis on friendship as a mutual relationship is an order determined by competition instead of equality, in which institutional structures – from multi-national societies to the psychological and social structures of the individual – are encrusted with a deep and general fear of friendship and love. Moreover friendship is denied by sexism, racism and the class system. Heyward sees the absurd climax of non-relationship in National Socialism, when through hatred of the Jews friendship and relationship led to the Holocaust. She finds the reactions to this in the writings of Eli Wiesel since, as she thinks, he stands for the absolute value of friendship.

Heyward ends her book with an appeal to messianic friendship, i.e. friends who do not wait for a heavenly Messiah but already represent in their personhood the transpersonal dynamics in the world.

Heyward has revived the old biblical notion of friendship with God, restored Jesus as friend to theology and introduced friendship as a comprehensive notion of mutual relationship which challenges all realms of relationships. But her own interest is focussed above all on the friends of Jesus who give God a body in the world and thus make a new morality possible. Since in English 'friend' is not gender-specific, it is possible to read both men and women friends out of the text.

Mary Hunt

In the course of the 1980s interest in feminist theology shifted to the significance of friendship itself, above all when women discovered specifically friendships between women and became critical of the often Aristotelian presuppositions according to which only men were capable of friendship. The decisive voice which championed a friendship which begins from friendship between women but sees this as an inspiration for all other forms of friendship, rather than an exclusive relationship, was that of Mary Hunt with her book *Fierce Tenderness. A Feminist Theology of Friendship.*[5]

As a lesbian feminist, Hunt sees a manifestation of fundamental humanitarian values and modes of behaviour in friendship between women. Such friendship is never named and is always hidden or discriminated against. As a result she also can speak of this discovery as a 'Copernican shift' in theology. She reports many friendships between women, known and unknown, and recognizes in them both political aspects and also religious dimensions which not least can take on life-sustaining significance in an age threatened by destruction. As a feminist theologian she starts from the experience of friendship between women, and in so doing touches critically on traditional theology and biblical positions. In contrast to her predecessors, for her the tradition of Jesus eating with toll collectors and sinners is not a major factor; indeed it is not even mentioned. Now the central saying about friendship from the Gospel of John, 'Greater love has no one than this, that he lays down his life for his friends', mobilizes her whole criticism of a Christianity fixated on the symbolism of death. Starting from friendship between women, for which sharing and joy in life with friends stands at the centre, she calls for a theology and ethics which is based on such values.[6] But Hunt wants to re-interpret the central metaphor of friendship in Christianity. She thinks that women would not put the death of a friend at the centre, but rather the survival of women. What would be more appropriate would be a metaphor from women's experience, e.g. the triumph of a group of women over unrighteousness which is achieved without losing one of them. Such a triumph would be a feminine history of resurrection. By contrast, the traditional Christian story is a male story which does not correspond to the vision of women but in fact opposes it.

Thus Hunt dissociates herself from what for her is a masculine Christian tradition or wants to rewrite it. Even friendship with God as a friend, whether envisaged as masculine or feminine, no longer plays any role for her. Instead of this she prefers to speak of friendship with the divine, which does not mean a person but different deities or friends. For Hunt, friends provide a rich and imaginative image which can develop and investigate the great diversity of the divine. She does not think that the image is perfect, but that it does help to bring people in touch with a personal and collective history, with negative and positive aspects.

If the Johannine saying about the love of a friend, which can mean dying for a friend, is torn from the biblical context, the suspicion could readily arise that in Christianity and theology itself friendship is fixated on death. But if the saying is put in the whole biblical context and interpreted in the light of the Synoptic account of the last supper, the lively aspect of this New Testament becomes visible. Friendship is realized by sharing a table, and it comprises those who suffer under injustice. This stands on its head the whole ancient concept of friendship, as being between males of equal status. It means a quest for justice, a concept which is important for Hunt's notions of friendship. It means open friendship, which also remains open for others who are marginalized.

The biblical image of friendship is not fixated on death. It is revolutionary, overturning the world of philosophy. It is focussed on life, life in justice. This overall view is lacking in Hunt's work, a view which first comprehends life in all its reality.

Hunt's theology of friendship is stimulating, militant and orientated on life, and in the notion of incarnation it finds the first steps towards embodiment and this-worldliness. But one asks whether here in the end we do not have the sketch of a feminist vision which has little to do with the Christian tradition and which also does not stand up to reality.

Hildegard Keul

In her book *Becoming Incarnate through Contact. Bettina Brentano-Arnim as a Pioneer of Feminist Theology*, Hildegund Keul takes quite another course.[7] She arrives at new insights into friendship which include both human relationships and also a religious dimension. Keul investigates the friendship between Bettina von Arnim and Caroline Günderode and interprets this relationship as friendship between women, although the term does not itself occur in the literature. By friendship between women she understands not only the process in which the women get together, but the creative way of dealing with the world which she calls touching, contact. This contact involves two things: the perception of one's own person and knowledge of the world in which this person lives. The self is not a solipsistic monad, but is not dissolved in relationships either. The person is changed by relationship and at the same time changes the relationships in which she lives. Keul sees such contact or touching as the basic concept of an 'ontology of the experience of God, human beings and the world'.[8]

Contact does not dissolve the polarity between the women. It takes place in both listening to one's own voice and listening to the voice of the other. The romantics created a new culture of relationships between women which contrasted with the Philistinism of their time.

Moreover, from such friendship between women there arises the idea of the foundation of a religion, a religion which makes people new. The language of love between the women friends arouses something unknown, is a new creation. And this language of love is ultimately the language of God. The kingdom of God is seen in this love. The new religion is to benefit humankind.

The result is the rejection of a theistic religion; however, 'the religion of hovering', as Bettina calls it, is not just immanent. It is about the transcendence in the immanence, which takes place in touching, whispering and speaking; experience with the world and involvement with one another.

So the relationship between the women friends is moulded by the priority of listening over speaking – a break with patriarchal tradition, which begins with uttering commands and ends with obedient hearing. In this new mutuality Keul recognizes a phrase of the American theologian Nelle Norton, who has described the new element in the relationship between women as 'hearing to speech'. Morton can see God in the metaphor of the listener or as the 'ear of the universe'. Keul describes this image of God as the one who listens passionately. But from the friendship between the two romantics she then comes upon the more appropriate image of God the woman friend: God the woman friend is the one who listens, just as the woman friend is the one who listens. In this way she can become a companion on the way to liberation: 'Where God hears a woman to speech, she becomes the friend of this woman.'[9] This metaphor has the power both to support and to reveal. God is different from what the traditional image of God teaches. God can be experienced in the experience of women friends, but is not dissolved in it.

Initially this image of God the woman friend has nothing to do with the biblical notions of friendship. It grows out of the protest against a prevailing culture of domination and speech, and develops among women who hitherto have been mute, condemned to obedience and listening. It reflects their own specific character and attaches less important to public characteristics, involving the senses. It takes on social significance for their own culture of human relationships and also a culture which goes beyond them, and it makes a claim to a transcendence which arises from love of and passion for the world. Here, however, aspects of the biblical images of God become visible: hearing and listening, mutuality, partnership, concern, unconditional love and unfailing interest. This recalls the Wisdom of God, which seeks men and women on their ways, finds them and supports them. With her discovery of God as woman friend Keul perhaps comes nearest to the images of God in wisdom, all of which offer the friendship of God.

Earthing friendship

If Moltmann is interested in the interpretation and reintroduction of the concept of friendship into theology through the demolition of social, but above all of ecclesiastical, hierarchies, in other words in new church fellowships, which also means a new understanding of the honorific christological titles, some years later McFague begins above all from ecological questions. She uses friendship as a new metaphor for the relationship between humankind and the earth. The basis for friendship is freedom, but this should not be misunderstood in individualistic terms. There must be a common interest, in this case the healing and well-being of the earth; there must also be mutual respect between the many and the different, whether these are the sexes, other forms of life, non-human or divine life. Finally, there must be maturity and responsibility.

For Carter Heyward it is important to give bodily form to God in the world through friends and friendships. Incarnation was not a one-off thing, but happens today in new ways through friends and friendship among men and women. Mutuality is the basic pattern for friendship and at the same time the basic pattern of the relationship between God and humankind. A revolutionary power will proceed from it.

For Hunt, friendship with women stands at the centre, a friendship which is 'impetuous and tender'. This friendship provides stimuli for reappropriating the symbols of the divine, ethical norms in dealing with other people, and meaningful attitudes towards animals and the earth. But above all, friendship between women provides an impetus for communities of friends who are in search of righteousness to engage in active reflection and reflective action with the aim of creating a more friendly world.

Keul is similarly interested in women friends who venture contact with one another and together shape their life. In order to change the world in line with their friendship, women begin where the patriarchate least wanted them to – with themselves. They change their understanding of themselves as helpless victims and resolve to take the way of the new creation. The guardian of the home becomes the creator of the world, which she learns to see in her own way, with her own eyes. So as friends women can commit themselves to the liberation of women and to justice. This brings them into conflict with the violence of the patriarchate, but also allows them to experience communities of resistance and solidarity.

In all five schemes there has been an exodus from a Christianity and from a theology which had been shaped by paternalistic images, which imagined God as standing over the world powerfully and in isolation, and which accordingly saw human beings as children, dependent and immature. Common to all are new patterns of behaviour, a new responsibility to the world and a clear view of the interdependence of all life on this earth. Common to the scheme of these women is that they do not divert into an abstract conceptuality, but are each earthed in new and unaccustomed ways. In theology we are accustomed to speak of incarnation – of God becoming human, being embodied. Earthing is a new vivid term for that.

What do such earthings actually look like?

McFague sees the world as God's body. That does not mean that she identifies God with the world, but she does recognize the relationship between God and the world in the human relationship of spirit and body. Human beings as worldly, corporeal beings thus live in the presence of God. From this could emerge a new understanding of the sacraments which again understood and celebrated the precious nature, the vulnerability and the uniqueness of the world.

Carter Heyward earths God, embodies God in God's friends.

For Hunt, earthing also takes place in the notion of embodiment, in which friendships take place, whether these are meals, physical contacts, shared actions, the acceptance of the history, the feelings, the experiences of others, or the pleasurable reappropriation of the body. For her the notion of incarnation therefore becomes an important Christian reminiscence, even if she can no longer derive a personal image of God from it.

Finally, for Keul contact is the central word for describing incarnation within friendship. It is an intensive relationship, for each other and on each another, which raises the other and oneself to life. In such friendship between women, God is experienced as the listener who prompts speaking, as the woman friend.

These diverse earthings seem to me to indicate the basis for an image of God as woman friend or a theology of friendship. Today they are possibilities of grasping the divine, of seeing in ourselves the way in which all life on this earth is interwoven and endangered, and of getting out of our own shadows as women. They form new bodily elements in a theology which is remote from the body. They stimulate us to experience incarnation, the embodiment of God, ourselves in hearing, touching, at meals, in bodily contacts, in the interplay of body and spirit, in actions.

We can now see what role women in particular play in concrete notions of friendship and how important images of friends in religion become for a world in which there are also other forms of life alongside the dominant family structures. And we can see how markedly such images regularly present themselves in the exposition of the Christian tradition. They can be helpful in supplementing and extending the many unsatisfactory parental images which perpetuate the status of children.

With the use of terms like friend and friendship, the notion of God as one who is close to us, as an ally, which is now being impressed on us but so far has been caught up in ideas of covenant, partnership, companion, takes on a living, warm intensity which extends into all our life and can earth us. We can experience friendship, among women and among men, with pleasure and sometimes also with pain. Here friendship with God is not a dogma but an offer to commit oneself anew to God, beyond all the poisoning of God, beyond all the domination, and to do so in the midst of our lives as woman or man, as child, mother, father and friend.

In the following chapters we shall go yet more deeply into the biblical notions which keep occurring. How is the death of

Jesus to be understood in the face of friendship with God? What significance does wisdom theology have here?

And above all, what can friendship mean, not only for women, but for theology, church and society?

In our day it is time to introduce into contemporary theological thought-patterns and into the social spheres of life insights into friendship, earthing, embodiment and contact which derive from the experience and reflection of women. In this way healing and healthy perspectives can be extended in both spheres.

3

Jesus, the Friend

Whereas in later feminist schemes friendship itself has come into the centre and Jesus the friend has lost significance, for me Jesus as friend has become important again. This development began during the critical reappraisal of the traditional understanding of the eucharist on which I worked with feminist theologians from Württemberg. The results of our work appeared in 1996 in a short study entitled 'We Women and the Lord's Supper'.[1] Like many women all over the world, here we opposed the deeply-rooted notion of sacrifice which lay at the basis of the eucharist. This was, first, because women too often down to the present day become victims and have internalized the behavioural patterns of victims. Secondly, it was because this notion is opposed to the understanding of God in feminist theology that God needs victims. In addition, voices were raised by a number of exegetes who read out of the New Testament only a very thin sacrificial interpretation, deriving above all from the late Letter to the Hebrews. This confirmed our critical attitude. We sought to progress from the image of a sacrificial death of Jesus which took place for our sins. I replaced sacrifice with the image of self-surrender, which includes not only passive suffering but also an element of self-determination. However, the passionate, indeed excessive, protest by many Württemberg male theologians, which was also supported by the church authorities, made it quite clear to me how deeply thought in terms of sacrifice is anchored not only in the eucharist but also in theology, in church structures and in Christian life, and governs its self-understanding

Dying for friends

On one occasion a woman asked me for another image of the death of Christ. That prompted me to take up for myself and for her the Johannine interpretation of the death of Christ, 'Greater love has no man than this, that a man lay down his life for his friends' (John 15.13).

In the past this sentence has often been misused and has been interpreted in terms of heroism. What can it say today?

Alongside other New Testament interpretations – ransom, substitution, redemption from the powers, etc. – the image of the love of a friend incorporates human experiences and can perhaps open up new approaches to images like sacrifice which have become incomprehensible. For me personally, friendship became a key to understanding yet other ideas which are theologically difficult to grasp: for example the relationship to God, long defined by 'sin'; and the relationship between father and child which so clearly has paternalistic features indicating dependence. Areas like earth, birth and body, which have fallen into the background or have even been defamed, can revive under the notion of friendship and be freed from the suspicion that they present nature religions. Time and again theology and the church have been accused of encouraging necrophilia under the sign of the cross. Now it can be demonstrated what a wealth of aspects there have been in the Christian tradition which are focussed on life and nature, and which can be developed in new directions.

Where are the roots for this motif? Elizabeth Schüssler Fiorenza connects this interpretation of the death of Christ with the New Testament formulae 'Christ died for . . .', which derive from Hellenistic Jewish ideas. According to the classical Greek tradition, friends died for their friends, soldiers for their nation and lovers for each other: 'This formula underscores the great value and high appreciation for people that is expressed in the messianic death of Jesus.'[2]

That this interpretation of the death of Jesus has something to say to women – as I have indicated above – has been energetically rejected by Mary Hunt.[3] She argues that women would not put the death of a friend at the centre of their religion, but the survival of women, and therefore it would be more appropriate to choose as a central symbol the triumph of a group of women in the struggle for justice – achieved without one of them being lost. So for her the death of Jesus as a friend comes from a male perspective.

If this statement about friendship is taken in isolation, such a suspicion may be justified. But the New Testament says other things about friends. These sayings are orientated on life and related to women and they fundamentally extend the image of Jesus the friend and change an apparently male symbolism. According to them Jesus first calls friends those who carry out what he has told them, who stand in a direct relationship to God and who are no longer 'slaves' (John 15.14f.). Lazarus and Judas also belong here. Then Jesus also picks up the malicious talk which is going the rounds about him, that he is a friend of prostitutes and sinners (Matthew 11.19; Luke 7.34); he opposes it, and thus also makes prostitutes and sinners friends. And according to our present-day knowledge, women also belonged in both groups. From the sources and from the many examples of meals of friendship, joyful gatherings at table which specifically included those who were apparently not friends, it can be inferred that here we have a description of a central practice of the Jesus movement. This is an image full of cheerfulness, joy in life; it is an unusual one and therefore was seen as scandalous. Where unusual pleasure is experienced at meals, people become mistrustful and envious: what is going on here?[4]

Who were these striking table companions? We know them under the description 'toll collectors and sinners', and have learned to associate immoral behaviour with these terms. But the expression does not simply describe a 'morally offensive group, but rather a class of people whose condition is so wretched that they had to engage in "disreputable" professions simply to survive'.[5] Feminist exegesis has demonstrated that this group included women as well as men, and therefore also speaks of both prostitutes and toll collectors in the feminine. The profession of toll collector was not an independent job, but involved being appointed to a toll office. Employees were often impoverished people and slaves of both sexes, with the usually unpleasant task of collecting tolls, which could be levied simply on a journey to the next place. The poverty of these employees led them to demand higher tolls, which meant that throughout antiquity their profession was regarded as deceitful and 'unclean'.

We should imagine prostitutes, too, to be included among sinners, women who for some reason had dropped out of the care provided by a patriarchal family and who therefore had to support themselves. According to the interpretation of the Torah by theologians they could be regarded as 'polluted' or 'unclean'. In my view, Mark also saw the story of the woman with a flow of blood in such a context, since he uses the same words to describe her precarious situation as those to be found in the Levitical commandments about cleanness (Mark 5.24–34; Leviticus 5.23ff.).

In contrast to other religions associations like the Essenes and the Pharisees, here – according to Schüssler Fiorenza – the ritual cleanness of the 'holy' table is not observed. It is not the cultic meal but the richly adorned table of a banquet which has become the symbol for the coming kingdom of God.[6]

So the outsiders of society, the marginalized, women as well as men, sat at this enjoyable table at which they could eat their fill: it contained not only bread and water but also wine, meat, fish, vegetables and other food. But for Jesus and his followers there was also the custom of eating at table together and having good meals with friends like Mary, Martha and Lazarus; an intimate meal was also held by the closest circle: the supper, which also included women.[7] So friendship was celebrated and practised in the Jesus movement at a great variety of tables, and in early Christianity the disreputable cry that Jesus was a friend of such often questionable groups became an honorific name: Jesus, the friend.

Wisdom's friendly meal

The primal image for this tradition of sharing a table with friends as described in the Gospels is to be found in Old Testament wisdom theology, and that once again indicates hidden feminine traditions of friendship. There Wisdom summons everyone from the streets to her richly adorned table:

> Wisdom has built her house, she has set up her seven pillars. She has slaughtered her beasts, she has mixed her wine, she has also set her table. She has sent out her maids to call from the highest places in the town, 'Whoever is simple, let him turn in here!' To him who is without sense she says, 'Come, eat of my bread and drink of the wine I have mixed' (Proverbs 9.2–5).

Here Jesus and Wisdom are seen in parallel: at the abundant meal there is fellowship; people eat their fill; there is understanding, comfort, renewal – a prefiguration of the banquets of the kingdom of God (Isaiah 25.6; Mark 14.25).

According to theological research, Jesus understood himself as Wisdom, and the earliest christology seems to have been a sophialogy.[8] For women, a feminine model emerges here which once again makes it easier for them to approach the story and the practice of Jesus: it is originally Wisdom whose significance and functions Jesus takes over. And it is important that Jesus' friendly action is expanded by Wisdom the householder, who issues an invitation, she is wine steward, butcher and cook. Here friendship takes on more life, becomes more concrete, practical, vital. If one asks oneself who prepared the meals for the group around Jesus, a realistic picture emerges here: it was the women, the women householders, who themselves had everything under control, and their women servants. And like Jesus Wisdom does not celebrate the meal with close friends but with those who are remote, strangers.

Did Jesus see himself as Wisdom? Did he identify with this female figure?

We may assume that according to Luke 7.35 he justified his friendly meals with the outcast by Wisdom, who recognizes all Israelites as her children.

It seems important to me that behind the great idea of sharing a table the reality of the household and housework also emerges. Today it encourages women to share meals and organize celebrations.

But this joyful gathering round the table, which we can also see in parallel to other famous gatherings round the table through history – Plato's symposium, the feast of the Grail, had just one social error which proved disastrous. It did not bring together close friends of the same class and the same sex, for a friendly meal, but those who were not friends. That was an offence against society and its rites. That forced accusations against the one who initiated them and finally led to his death. So he did not die for our sins but for those women and men who had been his friends, for friendship as a passionate human relationship and liberation.

If the criterion of true friendship is mutuality, we must ask whether such a mutual giving and taking really exhausts the relationship between Jesus and his friends. The sources at our disposal are the Gospel narratives about Jesus' relationship to his disciples, men and women. Carter Heyward fails to find in the Gospel of Mark, of which she makes a special investigation, reports of such mutuality in Jesus' friendships which caused particular joy. She believes that the authors of the Gospels were wrong about the key point of the passion of Jesus – that is, its roots in relationship. So she wants to portray a Jesus full of joy in human relationships, who knew that he had purely human

motives, as they did: a longing for intimacy, for reciprocal
intimate dealings with the world and other men and women.
Perhaps she asks too much of Jesus' relationships by loading
wishes for the present on to them. But it seems to me that
particularly in a new reading of the Gospels there is a series of
indications that here we do not have a Lord making contact
with his subjects; he was also dependent on them, learned from
them and needed their love and care. However, the mutuality of
the relationship becomes particularly clear only in the stories
about Jesus and women.[9] Here Jesus visibly learns something
from women: it is the Syro-Phoenician woman who makes him
understand that his is a mission to all men and women, and he
agrees with her image of the richly-decked table; in the anointing he experiences a kindly act and a prediction of his fate; by
Martha he is driven to raise Lazarus; the woman with a flow of
blood makes him feel the powers that are in his body. And at
the same time the women receive something from him: teach-
ing, experiences, stories, meals and unexpected affection. Their
journey to the tomb on Easter morning is then the conclusion of
a long mutual relationship which does not end even in death.
These relationships with women may lack a degree of cheerfulness, but they also lack tragic and ascetic features.

But in any friendship there are also experiences of otherness
and loneliness. At this point feminist theology sometimes seems
to me to think of relationship in too rigid terms. Thus for Rita
Nakashima Brock, who understands the relationship between
Jesus and the women as an erotic 'Christa/community', Jesus
was never completely abandoned, although his feelings are
depicted as abandonment by God. She writes:

Jesus does not die totally abandoned, though he is described
as feeling godforsaken. The divine erotic power illuminated
through Christa/Community in Galilee and the woman at
Bethany is sustained through Jesus' death by those who
watch him die and mark his burial site.[10]

Thus the story of Jesus runs the risk of being dissolved in a history of relationships. Community, friendship swallow up all individuality. Jesus' own story disappears. The values of the relationships stand in the forefront of interest. So in other schemes Jesus becomes one among many, the martyr like other martyrs, the crucified alongside many others who were crucified. He is then a friend among friends, and what happens is no longer an event in his life but an event in the life of his friends.

Such efforts represent an attempt to rob the story of Jesus the hero and the salvation brought by him of its power; they also play down the problems which some women have with the male redeemer and rediscover redeeming forces in the power of mutuality. That also explains why in the later schemes presented by feminist theologians, while friendship is investigated, Jesus as a friend is no longer of interest.

However, where that happens the personal relationship to a friend gets lost: this friend can also be different from me, and his or her history is not taken up in mine. But in this other story I can also recognize an experience of God which is more intensive and liberates me to a greater degree than I have perhaps ever experienced before. Here the friend remains someone over against me and thus a friend. We should meet the fear that there is in feminist theology about proclaiming the uniqueness of Jesus, the fear of a Christian claim to domination, not just politically, but also with the statements which women make in faith.[11]

The friend in everyday life

In contrast to such Western-feminist schemes, women in Africa still have a direct and existential interest in Jesus as friend. According to Doris Strahm's investigation, this notion of friendship is a 'notion of Christ which is near to the people', one of the most popular images among African women 'because they most need such a personal friend, and this image of Christ

helped them to endure their grief, their loneliness and their suffering'.[12]

According to Mercy Oduyoye, the Christ of African women
is 'above all a friend and companion who meets them in their
daily life, conquers the powers of death which destroy life, and
frees women from the burden of patriarchal prejudices and
oppressive cultural customs'. So he is a friend in the deepest
humiliation, but also a friend in self-affirmation.[13]

For African women too, the foundation is provided by the
Bible with its narratives about the friendship of Jesus with the
marginalized. Jesus does away with the blood taboos which are
also a burden to the African woman. He is a friend, comrade,
companion of these marginalized women and is thus also
regarded as a sympathetic friend in his public action. However,
his meaning is not limited to being 'friend and companion'. He
is also mother, wife, African woman, who in his humanity also
reveals the full being of a woman. Moreover, as suffering Christ
he is also the compassionate companion who is with women in
their situation of suffering while at the same time showing that
suffering is not in accordance with God's plan. The image of the
compassionate Jesus at the same time contains an invitation to
active solidarity which does not stop at identification with the
sufferers but leads to the restoration of life.[14]

If Jesus as friend is sometimes disappearing from Western-
feminist schemes, the relationship with Jesus as friend and its
rich tradition is once again regaining its power among African
women. The notion of Jesus as friend is not private consolation
for the soul but supports women through every situation in life,
through everyday existence and suffering, through new beginnings and resistance. In our own culture, something like this
notion of friendship encouraged the mystics to think for themselves; it made Teresa of Avila act independently and supported
Louise Otto-Peters' new beginning for women.[15]

Where does such friendship have a place in our present-day
theological models? For me Wisdom theology is permeated by

such a supportive friend. Wisdom is like a friend (Proverbs 7.4) who calls people to her, accompanies them along their ways – and, for me one of the finest expressions of her nature is that she goes with Joseph down the well, into all human and divine forsakenness, and does not abandon him (Wisdom 10.13). As in Wisdom's invitation to share her table, here is a prefigurement of the existential theology of the cross.

The image of the friend opens up parental images of God which often have connotations of dependence. Jesus himself was no dependent, obedient son. On the contrary, he was very critical of his own family of blood relations; he regarded his disciples, men and women, and his friends, men and women, as his family.[16] One ideal of early Christianity was the *familia dei*, the family of God, a community which is not constituted through ties of blood but is voluntary and constituted by friendship.

However, the image of the friend does not suppress the images of parents, as the Bible and our examples show; to the trust and security of parental images it adds above all friendly freedom and support. It replaces the notions of redemption which have often become incomprehensible with human, everyday notions. As Wisdom theology shows, it can also be interpreted in feminine terms. Its functions are hardly those of encouraging morality and providing an example; rather, it opens up a broad area of life in which love and detachment, freedom and security, are the basic pattern.

If Jesus' practice of sharing meals is one of the most important elements in his life and activity, it is amazing that in the light of Jesus, who is experienced here so centrally as a friend, no christology of friendship has ever developed. It is also amazing how few open brotherly and sisterly or messianic friendships have so far stamped the face and the thought of Christianity. A friend too can heal and forgive. Friendship too can liberate and transform.

Where are there known and hitherto concealed traces of such

a notion of friendship in earliest Christianity, in which the unconditional and all-inclusive love of God is earthed? I want to investigate these questions in the following chapters.

4

The Last Supper as a Meal of Friendship

What today binds us most intensively to Jesus' action as a friend could be the eucharist. What could make the eucharist once again more lively and physical would be to celebrate it as a meal of friendship. Nowadays women often unconsciously foster such traditions. They meet, cook and eat together, strengthen and support one another in the midst of their every-day surroundings and everyday conflicts, and have developed rituals of intimacy and contact. But many people still experi-ence the traditional celebrations of the eucharist as rituals in which mourning, death and sin stand in the foreground. Such celebrations are stamped with the notion that Jesus died a sacri-ficial death on the cross for our sins. The liturgy, gestures, eucharistic hymns emphasize this basic mood, which is already introduced in many confessions by the confession of sins that stands at the beginning of the service. And in the Catholic eucharist there are the words, 'Lord, I am not worthy . . . '[1]

By now changes have been made in many congregations: the confession of sins has been dropped, sorrowful eucharistic hymns have been replaced by cheerful songs of fellowships, and the mood has become more relaxed. But anyone who looks more closely will notice that deep down in the eucharistic ritual there is still a christology that is stamped by sacrifice.

How is it possible to replace the notion of atoning sacrifice with that of the death of a friend and an act of friendship, and thus also free one's own life from the mentality of sacrifice?

How is it possible in the eucharist not only to attain powers of forgiveness and again to 'come clean' with oneself (which is how many understand it), but also experience powers of life which transform us, which open up our narrow limitations?

For this to happen, different steps need to be taken. It is possible to leave behind the understanding of a sacrificial death which is deeply engraved on the Christian consciousness. But that in no way means setting aside the biblical tradition in order to install simply a cheerful meal among Christians. Rather, in our critical steps we come across biblical traditions which Western Christianity has often missed.

If we put the statement 'Greater love has no man than this, that he lays down his life for his friends' (John 15.13) at the centre of a eucharistic celebration, and understand this sentence – as the New Testament does – in close connection with the narratives about the friendly meals that Jesus had with the outcast and abandoned of an 'intact society', there is no longer any room for a confession of sins in which I declare myself to be poor, wretched and sinful. Those who are invited to such a meal first experience respect and dignity there. They are filled, but there they experience not only what being full is, but also a sense of well-being through food and drink which are not everyday food and drink. Those who have this experience are happy, rather than being conscious of their sins.

In such a meal, which is built up on the tradition of the friend, there is a place for a confession or a prayer of happiness and gratitude, gratitude for liberation for friendship with God and fellowship with God. We can also reflect at it that time and again we ourselves are such outcasts: sick, helpless people who now experience acceptance, healing and power. Such a process is important for women in particular, since – as we shall go on to see – for many of them guilt is a basic feeling and they often find it difficult to feel that they are somebody, with a body which is right and an existence which is good, whole and beautiful.

It is the task of such a celebration of friendship to raise people up, to give them confidence in themselves and in God; to liberate them in the community from fears, loneliness and a sense of being torn apart.

Self-surrender instead of sacrifice

A further step would be to liberate ourselves from the remnants of thinking in terms of sacrifice which slumber deep in Christian thought and which, as René Girard says, pollute the innermost recesses of our brains.[2] A sacrifice usually presupposes guilt and damage. It comes about through violence and means a loss of life and blood. Notions of sacrifice give rise more to a mentality of sacrifice than to a responsible healing action.

Girard has demonstrated that the Gospels never speak of sacrifice 'except to exclude it'. Granted, in the Gospels the passion is depicted as an act which is to bring people salvation, but never as a sacrifice. The 'sacrificial interpretation of the passion' is 'the most paradoxical and colossal misunderstanding of the whole story'.[3]

However, notions of sacrifice have slipped into Christian life and thought partly because they correspond to current religious notions and partly because they meet the human need for a scapegoat, for ritual resolutions of conflicts.

We can replace sacrifice with the term self-surrender, which at first hearing sounds similar. But in contrast to sacrifice, self-surrender is an act of one's own free will; it is bound up with responsibility and love, and is interested in the preservation of life.

According to the Gospels, Jesus' life is stamped by such self-surrender, and death comes only at its end. Those who abandon thinking of the eucharistic action in terms of sacrifice can attempt to understand Jesus' life anew as a life of self-surrender. Jesus healed people, raised them up, put them in the immediate presence of God and made them friends of God. However, he did not just do something, but gave himself and his whole person in this process, not from self-denial and a sacrificial mentality but out of free love. This message, these gestures of friendship which surround his person and actions, were to a considerable degree critical of society, because they led the existing conditions of domination to a state of collapse. They provoked the wrath of the guardians of the law, and that finally cost Jesus his life. But death had not been his purpose; it was the consequence of his life.

The question is whether in that case we can speak of sacrifice at all. There will always be victims of violence in unjust conditions, victims of oppression and tyranny, who rightly see their role as victims reflected in the 'sacrifice' of Christ.

From a distance, Jesus' death too can be regarded as the death of the victim of a brutal exercise of power. But these external aspects should not be internalized.

According to Hans Kessler, if we can use the concept of sacrifice in Christianity at all, we can use it only if it is changed in such a way that it is stamped by Jesus' total loving self-surrender to the Father and us – a giving of himself which takes place out of self-affirmation, not out of self-denial or a desire for sacrifice.[4]

Such self-surrender out of self-determination can become part of the message of the eucharist, clarified by stories and texts, and that should challenge us to our a life of our own which is self-determined and responsible.

Now self-surrender is no attraction to many women; sacrifice and self-surrender are often confused, and in feminist discussion they have been condemned as passive masochistic behaviour in the face of sadistic domination. The cross, the crucified Jesus, the theology of the cross, have become examples of a religious mentality of sacrifice which had been commended to women in particular. It is here that feminist theology has developed its strongest theological aggressiveness, but at the same time it has also banished from its language and thought all modes of behaviour like acceptance, tolerance, suffering, self-surrender, endurance and humility. This process continues, but now suspicious voices are also being raised, reclaiming the cross and the theology of the cross for their own existence and the crosses which are caused by society.

Christian men and women need not read a delight in suffering, sado-masochism and a sacrificial mentality out of Jesus' death; it is a model of freely chosen dedication or self-surrender.

That could make human life more relaxed and more resolute.

The life-giving body of Jesus

A further problem is how we are to understand the body of Christ which is given to those who are guests at the eucharistic as bread or wafer; traditionally this is understood as the body of the one who died for us, which is given for us. Do not all attempts to revitalize the eucharist struggle at this point?

In fact the biblical eucharistic texts seem to confirm the images of death. But a closer look at the Gospel of Mark, which has always been a source of new feminist discoveries, shows us something else. Here the words of interpretation at the Last Supper, which are the briefest in the New Testament, also allow of another interpretation. In them we read:

'Take, eat, this is my body.'
'This is my blood of the new covenant
which is shed for many.'

So we do not have the 'for the forgiveness of sins' which causes offence to many people; these occur only in Matthew. Nor do we have the 'for you', which Luke inserts, and which suggest our responsibility for the death of Jesus. Thus two elements are lacking from which the global understanding of sins and the notion of the atoning death of Jesus bound up with it can be derived and can still be heard. In the context of the Gospel of Mark the words of interpretation have another reference.

The word 'body' is twice used for the body of Jesus. It is used first when the unknown woman anointed the body of Jesus with precious oil: this can be understood as the anointing of a prophet and king and an anointing for death (Mark 14.8), and Jesus says of it that the woman has come to anoint his body 'for his burial'. The word 'body' also occurs at the burial (Mark 15.43). The notion of the dying, sacrificed body could develop from these two mentions. If we understand the words of institution from these two aspects, there really is only the image of death.

But the same word 'body' is also used in Mark for the body of the woman who has touched Jesus' robe (which means Jesus himself, for the material is identical with the body – Leviticus 15) and as a result has felt dynamic forces in her body that have healed her from her torment (Mark 5.29). Here body is understood as a sound, healed body. The body of Jesus is also mentioned indirectly in this context, for he felt something like a dynamic, i.e. an energy, which 'went out of him' (v.3). So here there is the thought of a bodily communication which goes out of a highly vital human body and passes over to the sick body of the woman, who is dying for loss of blood. There is an exchange of bodily energy which gives the body of Jesus a different significance from that of a dying or dead body.

Perhaps here we have a Hellenistic notion of the bodily effectiveness of the miracle-worker. Be this as it may, for theology and theologians such an effective power emanating from the body of Jesus is terrifying. Eduard Schweizer thought that this scene was described in a shockingly physical way,[5] and the later Gospels already no longer depicted the dynamic of this process. That Jesus' body was also a healing body is no longer noted in a christology orientated on death and resurrection.

'This is my body' – this saying at the Last Supper thus refers to the healing, life-giving body of Jesus. Thus the supper in Mark deliberately recalls his bodily action. Accordingly, redemption takes place not only through his death but also through his life, which touches on others.

Mark's second word of interpretation, 'This is my blood of the new covenant which is shed for many', shows for whom Jesus will die. Mark calls them the *polloi*, the many. According to the exegesis of the Korean New Testament scholar and liberation theologian Ahn Byung-Mu, these are not just any people.[6] Nor is *polloi* the expression for a universalistic notion of humankind; it refers to the *ochlos* (Greek for crowd), which followed Jesus and was dedicated to him in partnership. *Ochlos* comprises the sinners, toll collectors, sick, lepers, prostitutes – all those who have professions or are in situations which have forced them to the edge of society. 'They were sinners because they transgressed the law or could not adapt to the law. From this standpoint social sin and religious alienation were in reality two sides of one and the same coin.'[7] According to Mark it is for them, these outcasts, that Jesus has come. He has given his life for these friends, not, as in our moralistic church misunderstanding, for sinners.

These two observations on the Markan eucharistic words show that the Last Supper in Mark is a meal which again makes present in eating together the life-giving energy that has been experienced. Just as this energy has brought back the woman from death to life, so too in the eucharist it can again make people certain and sure of their bodies.

All the outcast are included in this meal of friendship. For our celebration of the eucharist, that means that in them should be remembered all those who at present are socially, economically or psychologically in the shadows, e.g. single parents, addicts, the unemployed, the old, the asylum-seekers. But it also includes all those who exclude something in themselves which is part of their whole personality: for women often their capacity for thought, for men more their feelings. Celebrations of the eucharist could again bring us in touch with the whole of our conflictual life in the present.

Theogusty – tasting God

One last good step would be to make it possible again to experience the eucharist with the senses. For this, it would be helpful to see the celebration which has found its way into a sacrificial corner once again in connection with the many meals that Jesus had with the most diverse people, in large and small groups. And these meals not only satisfied them but also gave them pleasure. They tasted good. They included not only life-sustaining bread, but also fish, vegetables, lamb, wine and presumably many other good things. These were everyday experiences which were associated with the feeling of happiness, satisfaction, pleasure and vital strengthening.

Not every one of our meals is a supper. But every meal can reflect something of a such a supper. Heinrich Böll spoke of the sacramental cup of tea, and women ask whether the kitchen table would not be the appropriate place for the supper, the table at which women prepare the countless life-sustaining meals which also give life its pleasure.[8]

The question is how we again make bread and wine, wafers and juice, so tasty, or how we communicate by taste that we can taste and see how friendly God is. For with the elements God's life, the power and courage of life, enter into our body. So I would want to speak of a sacred materiality through which our insecure, torn, abused bodies can again detect acceptance, concern and fellowship. However, I do not understand this as holiness in the sense of a transubstantiation of transformed elements. The elements are holy only in so far as they are accepted with all our senses and our whole person and accompany us back into society and everyday life.

The meaningful and sensual way in which we celebrate the

supper also sheds a light on our eating habits and our under-standing of the body. If eating serves only to sustain power to go on competing, hardly anything holy can be detected in it. If the body is the vehicle which has to kept healthy, and no more, no transcendence will become visible in the eating.

Jutta Anna Kleber, the sociologist of medicine, has demon-strated very well this break between two different concepts of body and eating by means of Augustine and Hildegard of Bingen.[9]

In Augustine the feeding of the body exclusively serves to sus-tain it. Eating is necessary and a duty for Christians. Fasting and continence must not endanger health. However, for Augustine the wisdom of eating is not orientated on the equi-librium of body, soul and spirit but on the emancipation of the spirit from the body. In this way he has left a basic stamp on the West and its relation to the bodily dimension.

In the last resort nourishing does not serve to equip the body but inwardly to equip the soul. The body indeed remains the basis for knowledge and ecstasy, but knowledge and ecstasy have a transcendent tendency which leaves the body behind.

Hildegard of Bingen differs. For her, earthly health is the centre of life. Here alone the numinous nature of the holy is experienced. In her view the material constitution of the food transforms the coarse material of the body into finer bodily material. For her, eating and drinking lead the body directly on the way to God. Religious ecstasy is then 'an emergence from everyday involvement in the split in the primal ground of unity, i.e. a process of experiencing which enters the body', whereas in Augustine it is precisely the tendency to leave the body which stamps ecstasy and brings the split to a climax. If in Augustine eating constantly poses a danger to the process of human spiri-tualization, in Hildegard eating and drinking are 'a catalyst for the spiritual'. If in Augustine a hatred of the body and material nature are evident, Hildegard has the vision of a unity of spirit and body in the human being which are to be regained.

Kleber also investigates the view of the eucharist in both writers and comes to the following conclusion:

Whereas in Augustine transubstantiation in the eucharist always transcends the bodily nature of human beings at one point, in Hildegard the nourishment brings about a continuous process of life, which refines the bodily energy and makes it more subtle, with a view to the purity of the paradisal body which can be regained.[10]

Hildegard's way did not become the way of the West. But it could become so again if we overcome the old divisive hatred of body and matter, rediscover God and the divine in them, and celebrate the eucharist as a place where our threatened body and the endangered creation are again perceived and experienced in their holiness. This would be the way to a sacramental understanding of the kind that McFague visualizes (see above, p. 29).

In bread and wine we can taste God – Kurt Marti used the term 'theogusty' here[11] – and keep hope alive on this earth in the face of all apocalyptic prophecies.

If we experience the eucharist in a sensual way, the sparse elements change, the body that we have set aside becomes loveable, the earth again becomes our home and the creation the place of our commitment. In the eucharist, friendship with God brings us right up against the body – liberating us and challenging us.

But what prevents people from tasting God and experiencing God with all their senses?

At this point we have to reflect anew on the nature of sin.

5

Separation from God and Goodness

Various notions of sin go along with Christianity and paralyse it, but provide the legitimation for the existence of some churches and theologies. However, many people feel overwhelmed with talk of sin and guilt, and are weary of the calls coming from all sides to acknowledge guilt. They feel that this spread of taking the blame is Christian arrogance which can even become oppressive. But theology and churches maintain the fatal and unbiblical doctrine of original sin that once served to justify state and church control of a humanity which was thought to be helpless.

How can such a culture of guilt still be maintained in the face of the friendship of God which the Bible promises us?

What does sin look like if Jesus no longer died for our sins, but gave his life for his friends out of friendship?

How can what so long was burdened with the word 'sin', by which I mean our relation to God, now be seen under the aspect of friendship with God?

I would like to replace the word 'sin' with the words 'separation from God and goodness'. For me this implies that human beings can separate themselves from God morally and deliberately, but also fall away from the experience of goodness and well-being through fate, disaster and sickness. At all events it is important that we abandon our narrowly individualistic concept of sin and see the perverse side of our life as a departure from the community of creation, which for the individual means a loss of wholeness. However, wholeness is not to be understood as perfection, but dynamically. As Rose Ausländer put it, it is to be wounded in every part yet remain whole.

Even in feminist theology people keep falling into traps, have unclear concepts of wholeness, or even attack it. But I myself would like to begin from the holistic approach, which convinces me, and demonstrate ways out of the culture of guilt by the approaches from women's experiences.

Women's experiences

Particularly in recent years, women have begun to look critically on global and sweeping confessions of sin. The latter distort the relationship which women have discovered with God and the divine, and contradict their newly awakened understanding of themselves. But women do not simply regard themselves as whole and complete – a charge often made against them from the male side. On the contrary, women are highly sensitive to their guilt. How does this sensitivity present itself?

According to the psychologist of an urban nerve clinic, for many women 'a guilt feeling is the basic evil of human existence'. Far more than men, they excuse themselves, offer explanations, ask for understanding, seek the causes of all evil primarily in themselves. 'I learned the feeling of guilt in my earliest childhood years,' reported a woman. 'I felt so guilty if I had defended myself. I think that I was uncannily timid in my resistance as a girl during puberty.' Luise Rinser recalls that, 'All my education was aimed at making me quiet and docile, belittling myself, always having a sense of guilt which could not be put into words, always having to ask for forgiveness.'[1]

The network and relationships in a woman's existence are almost fated to make her responsible for others. There are the children, whose success or progress in life or whose failure is made dependent on the mother, though she is blamed more for their failure than credited with their success. There are the elderly parents, above all the old mother, for whom all too often the daughter has to take responsibility. She has to keep in touch with her mother and look after her, while this sense of obligation is never paramount between sons and old parents. And there are still men for whom the woman is the scapegoat for everything in the house that does not function.

This diffuse sense of responsibility and guilt can then often be repeated in work situations and within groups.

If this guilt feeling coincides with church norms, it can be reinforced. A woman's sense of guilt and the church's confession of sin can fuse in a fatal way and have often led to neurotic, self-tormenting behaviour. A woman wrote to me recently:

> From my childhood on (I was born in 1940), I have suffered over the theme that Jesus died for my sins – my guilt. At that time I identified completely with this statement of the churches; I eventually experienced it as my most personal fault as a child and (at the age of five or six) accepted it. I sought out my guilt, confused my disobedience with it, and among other things saw this disobedience as a cause of the guilt. My feelings led me to conclude that my existence wasn't right, or that my guilt was (is) my existence.
>
> I have 'learned' theology, and since then have been given 'adult answers', but for the child in me and for school-children the sayings about the cross have remained: the way in which they are formulated, their content and their threat, above all in the liturgy, in prayer and in hymns.

How do guilt and sin appear to women who arrive at a new sense of self-esteem? How do women get out of the vicious circle of always feeling guilty? How do they free themselves from church norms which apparently ignore their lives?

Many male concepts of sin start from the desire of human beings to be like God. Hybris, arrogance, is one of the most common definitions of sin. Underlying it is an understanding of God and deity which human beings can never live up to but which they may also never reach.

God can be understood as that which is absolutely true and good, which human beings can never live up to.

God and his commandments can be understood as so impossible to fulfil that human beings appear only as disobedient men and women.

God can be believed to be so fundamentally opposite to human beings that self-acceptance, self-redemption, self-love become the basic sin.

Women are increasingly having difficulties with such theological notions of sin. They have begun to recognize that they do not at all want to be like God, that they cannot even be themselves. Women are beginning to love themselves, and for self-love it is important to accept oneself.

So from a feminist perspective sin is precisely the opposite of hybristic arrogance. It is perverse, and contrary to God as friend, for women to belittle themselves and make themselves invisible, not to base themselves on the greatness and wholeness willed by God. It is perverse for them not only not to love but also to hate, for them not to realize the creation which God has brought about in them, so that they are not living in friendship with God.

An American, Valerie Saiving Goldstein, was the first to sense something of this different woman's sin when in 1962 she wrote that the specific feminine forms of sin have a quality which can never be described with terms like pride and a striving for power. They can be understood better if one speaks of triviality, distraction, long-windedness, a lack of concentration and dependence on others in one's own self-determination. Women go for tolerance at the cost of making demands, are unable to respect the limits of the private sphere; are sentimentality and fond of gossip; they mistrust the mind. In short in women the self is underdeveloped or negated.[2]

Valerie Saiving Goldstein went on to say that a woman can become nothing, almost a zero, with no intrinsic value, for herself, her fellow human beings or perhaps even for God.

I want to develop this approach further and begin from a holistic view of the human being which is not in principle permanently damaged, as happens with the doctrine of original sin, by talk of the 'fallen creation', and is also intimated by the term 'unmerited grace' which is continually cropping up.[3] Sin is a disruption of relationships in which the loss of wholeness and the damaging of our wholeness is evident. We are not 'whole' in our persons. We are not undivided and free from rifts in our relationship to nature and the world. What was meant to be whole, healthy, right, open and rich in relationships is perverted, stunted, twisted. People exclude something which belongs to them as God's whole, good creation. Women forget their selves, and often develop their whole personality only anxiously and with great difficulty. They constantly feel that they are torn apart into many pieces. Men tend more towards a greater sense of the self, to hybris. They put a strain on their supposed wholeness, exploit and misuse it.

A Swedish woman has demonstrated what for many women today is their 'sin' in an impressive 'confession of sins'. She writes:

Are there not sometimes other sins
to confess than these
which we have talked people into having?
Christ, I confess before you
that I have had no faith in my own potential.
That I have shown contempt for myself and my ability
in thought, word and deed.
I have not loved myself as much as others,
my body, my appearance,
my talents or my way of being myself.
I have let others guide my life.
I have let myself be scorned and mistreated.
I have relied more on the verdict of others
than on my own,

and I have allowed people to be indifferent
and malicious to me,
without telling them to stop.

I confess
that I have not developed to the fullest measure of my
     capacities,
that I have been too cowardly
to venture to argue for a just cause;
that I have wounded myself
in order to avoid controversies.

I confess
that I have not dared to show
how competent I am,
have not dared to be as competent
as I really can be.
God, our Father and Creator,
Jesus, my Brother and Redeemer,
Spirit, our Mother and Comforter,
forgive me my self-contempt,
raise me up, give me faith in myself
and love of myself.

                                        Lena Malmgren

So here 'sin' is a lack of self-love; it is self-contempt. But love
of self and contempt of self are precisely what are attacked
down to the present day in some ecclesiastical confessions of sin
as godless self-seeking. However, the Swedish woman discloses
women whose sense of being children of God and friends of
God has been buried. She discloses her lack of self-confidence,
her inability to develop her abilities, to see her body, to resist
injustice, to fight for a good cause. Unselfish, quiet, modest,
seeking peace, obsessed with harmony, assimilated – those are
the feminine sins which for all too long were feminine virtues.
In the background of this new confession of sin there is not a

theory of universal original sin, but the notion of a creation which is woman, who only now is seeing the light of day.

However, we have to ask whether this 'confession of sin' does not again fall into the old trap of guilt and orientate itself on an ideal of perfection behind which there is an absolute divine claim. This time the ideal would be one of a woman who always offers resistance, makes requests, is not assimilated, and is under the pressure of a new morality. It would be more helpful to begin from a human wholeness which includes all imperfections, damage and longings, and on the basis of such an incomplete wholeness to speak with God as with a friend.

Complicity

After the first beginnings of a new self-assessment, critical voices have been raised among feminists. It is said that with their new view of themselves, many women are caught up in egocentricity and individualism, and forget the political dimensions of the oppression of women. The quest for totality and femininity has been mistrusted; it is thought to distract attention from the political and social complicity of women. Complicity means that there is a more lively interest in the civilized patriarchates, so that women do not betray, fight or hinder men in their actions. 'We have become accomplices,' writes Christina Thürmer-Rohr, 'when we have adapted ourselves to ideas that we supplement men . . . when women support and protect the male individual by structuring their areas of responsibility – especially those of the home, of "social thinking" and "humanity" – in such a way that the male is freed for his activity.' Women were such accomplices in the Third Reich, in colonial exploitation and still are in the present-day destruction of the environment. Women are not victims of patriarchal power. For Thürmer-Rohr women do not 'create meaning', do pastoral and social work, gather scraps of spiritual or mystical thought, 'scratch around' in world history

in search of identifications, orientate themselves on strong
women of the past. Femininity is 'colonialized'; it is not an
alternative utopian form of society. She says that we have this
patriarchal colonization in our heads like a suppurating boil. It
is a good thing to recognize it, to make it innocuous and to see
how we live without it. The important thing is to live 'proudly
and helplessly', to bid farewell to faith, love and hope, and to
concentrate on the life that remains to us. 'It would be a revolutionary act if women could finally become nihilists in this
sense.' From illusions, the way must lead to dis-illusionment.[4]

For some feminist theologians there is a fascination in this
existentialist nihilism. The radicalism of the revolution in earliest Christianity recurs here. Any compromise is godless. In this
context, Hedwig Meyer-Wilmes can write of 'rebellion on the
frontier'. For others, having no place, no utopia, is the slogan:
the only way seems to be to persist in uncompromising and
critical protest.

Christa Mulack has expressed harsh criticism of this concept
of 'complicity'. The title of one of her books, *And Once Again
I Feel Guilty*, refers to the new attributions of guilt by women
which are now coming from feminists in particular.[5] These
attributions of guilt ultimately indicate a scorn of women and
can be understood only against the background of the Protestant culture of guilt. Now Mulack in no way rejects guilt as such.
On the contrary, for a person to acknowledge guilt is a sign of
maturity. But she cannot agree with the presuppositions which
with 'complicity' led to the attributions of guilt that are now
being made. These attributions of guilt come from a patriarchal
society of law and customs, without taking note of the value-
system of women at that time. Moreover they start from a freedom of decision which in the past women often did not have at
all. It must also be noted that women who thought and acted
independently were often regarded as abnormal; now this old
accusation of guilt cannot be turned round and used against
them. 'The price for our capacity for guilt would accordingly be

the suppression of our lack of conformity, which on the other hand is made a charge against women.'

For Mulack, the presuppositions for attributions of guilt are:

the possibility of insight into the injustice of particular conditions;

the possibility and the capacity to live without these conditions;

the freedom and power to change them.

Only when these three presuppositions have been changed, may there be talk of guilt among women. Otherwise attributions of guilt do not have the goal of emancipation and totality, but are simply an instance of the well-known hostility to women.

So Mulack does not want to whitewash women; rather she calls for a greater sensitivity to women, their character and history. The involvement of women in the monstrosities of the Third Reich, the exploitation of the Third World, and the pollution of the environment must be described and seen in specific terms. It would be too easy just to stamp women as accomplices on an equal footing.

For me, Mulack's approach is important, first, because it begins from women themselves and attempts to reassess their involvement in world history without stealing out of history and creeping into a mystical corner.

Secondly, I think that Mulack's central criticism of the Protestant culture of guilt is important. Here women are again made invisible. Here things are levelled down and equal rights are practised at the wrong place.

Furthermore, in connection with Thürmer-Rohr's concept of complicity it should be noted that here a way is being pointed out for women – standing on the frontier, in nothingness, in disillusionment, hopeless – which seems to me both narrow and elitist. This way may be typical of pioneers and champions. This must be a challenge for intellectuals, but now it is also more. It is a game with ideas, with revolutions, with changes in the world which then still collapse, as we have already

experienced time and again in German history. It is not a way
for women who are struggling for their authenticity and their
independence in everyday life. It is not a way into reality, where
there are legitimate compromises, and retreats are allowed. It is
not a way of healing and becoming whole.

Moreover the spiritual supports for this way are not exactly
encouraging. Christian Schaumberg writes that she would
rather see herself as a 'monster' than as 'good, whole and
beautiful' – my proposal for women, to love and accept themselves with all that is negative and positive.[6]

Therefore a large number of the schemes for women in
feminist theology with its sharp analysis remain confused when
it comes to demonstrating any healing. Thus, for example, the
analyses of contempt for the body in the patriarchate are comprehensive and apt, but what a liberated body looks like, how it
presents itself and acts – that is almost always left open, as
women have learned the art of revealing but hardly that of positive thought. Here we come up against a dilemma of feminist
theology which is at the same time the dilemma of contemporary theology: to be strong and convincing in analysis, i.e. to
stand out in the culture of guilt, but hardly to find language for
ways out of this disastrous situation. The culture of guilt has
also put down its deep roots in feminist theology. How do we
get out of it?

How do we rediscover in a convincing way the faith, love and
hope that we have lost?

How do we find words which make contact with people,
ideas which address totality and support women on their own
way?

How do we get away from existentialist thinking to a process
which corresponds to the realities of our life and includes social
process in our responsibility?

Where women discover wholeness, body and a sense of self,
they by no means remain stuck in an individualistic circle. The
wholeness which is discovered has its cosmic side; the senses

which come alive again in the body develop political sensitivity; they touch on our sensual consciousness. Our sense of self arouses sensitivity to the many minorities which are barely perceived. The private is also the political.

Forgiveness and healing

First I would like to ask again what sin and a fundamental experience of disaster is in feminist theology. It is the oppression of one gender by the other, sexism, which has many parallels and consequences that manifest themselves in other forms of oppression, racism, the class struggle. To this 'sin' corresponds the notion of a just world

The passion of feminist theology corresponds to such notions from the social spheres. They are images of a whole society, of a kind that is all too often forgotten by a Christianity which did not see the dignity and self-determination of women, the poor and non-white races. They are notions with high moral claims, which were often expressed in moral appeals. They are ideas which have a high degree of expectation that individuals and societies can be changed.

But after twenty years of lively feminist theology, I have come to ask myself how far its lofty, social and moral concept extends to all questions and spheres of life. It is striking that the individual does not play a role, that women are seen as a collective, and that any view of individuality has disappeared. What is the relationship between independence and solidarity? Isn't the distinctive nature of the women as a person overlooked, but doesn't it play an immensely important role in the process of the feminist movement? What is a movement without the individuals?

It is also striking that the life of every woman still continues to be stamped by other disastrous experiences like sexism and injustice. What is the meaning of sickness and death? When Valerie (Saiving) came up against these questions in view of her own illness, she suggested more support from women, more social welfare.[7] But is this social solution adequate?

A terminally ill feminist theologian asked at the end, 'What use is feminist theology to me now?', and her reaction was very sobering. 'Rubbish!'

I think that individual women's experiences of disaster and helplessness belong in our experience of injustice and sin. Otherwise we could fall victim to the error that everything could be done socially. Sickness, grief, loneliness, death are experiences which go with women's lives, even if we have got one stage nearer a social utopia. The immanent thinking of feminist theology is a fascinating motive force which grasps and illuminates us and our reality. But this dynamic provides support only if it carries with it that bit of expectation which extends beyond our social existence.

That does not mean that we should move out of the social and political worlds of concepts and ideas presented by feminist theology. But we should enlarge them by dimensions of women's lives which belong to our totality. In our commitment to justice we can recognize our limitations and entanglements, so that we can escape the illusion that we can make our own happiness. We must recognize our sickness, which again makes us conscious of our bodies. We shall not be able to suppress pain and suffering. We cannot exclude failure and helplessness from our life and make 'sexism' alone responsible for them.

But at the same time we can also discover our bodies, love them, experience them as friends, as a field of energy extending over a tremendous area, as the place of our thinking and understanding. We will also again learn to seek the individual meaning of our life in them. And we can hope beyond death. Our Western consciousness which reflects on itself, stamped by thinking in terms of expiation and guilt, is then opened up to many other notions of life.

The community of women, the solidarity of women, are possibilities the energetic potential of which has hardly been explored; they can communicate more life than we have hitherto suspected and practised.

If we look back at the New Testament tradition of women, the view is confirmed of the multiplicity of experiences of disaster from which women come, to go forward liberated, healed and encouraged. The depression and raising up of a woman is made clear to us by the story of the woman bent double. The episode of the woman with a flow of blood depicts a woman suffering social, physical and even economic limitations. She can go away healed and integrated into society. The story of Jairus' daughter depicts the helplessness experienced by a girl who cannot get free of her parents and who awakens to a life of her own. The women taken in adultery is acquitted and sent to a new life.

In the New Testament, 'sin' is separation from God and goodness, and is manifested in many different phenomena like helplessness, depression and physical sickness. It is manifested in anxiety and loneliness. It means separation from the good life, from people, from God. But this sin is not forgiven in the New Testament – it is healed.

Erich Fromm has proposed that we should break through the Western circle of sin and forgiveness and that we would do better to speak of sickness and healing.[8] Given a restricted notion of sin and forgiveness which can be backed up by statements expressing the church's power and has led to moralistic misunderstandings, sickness and healing seems to me to be an appropriate image which responds to present experiences of disaster – particularly also on the part of women. This image does not make them irresponsible and immature, for healing is a process which begins in the sick person herself and introduces a way that leads her to a wider sphere which is more than individual physical health. 'Go in shalom,' says Jesus to the woman who has been healed, and that means into a society and a cosmos which is dependent on salvation and also waits for our healing.

Healing is a process in which a hurt is made good, in which the wounds close. Healing takes time. Hope grows in healing. Healing comprises the most varied dimensions of my personality, the senses, the organs, the consciousness. Healing renews a comprehensive sense.

By contrast, 'forgiveness' recalls a judicial statement which comes from outside or from above. It embraces the consciousness. It opens up free space. It releases me from the judgment. But what happens then?

We have long understood our relationship with God in forensic terms, and our liturgical language is still stamped with such juristic terms: justification, atonement, the forgiveness of sins, acquittal. But human beings in their totality, with body, soul and spirit, are not touched by this. I rediscover in the world 'healing' a physical, bodily language which also addresses the forgotten dimensions of our person. Forgiveness pronounces us free; healing makes us free.

I think that the notion of heaven could help us to expand our current notion of forgiveness, which is too closely associated with legalistic thinking, and which focusses on individualism and a God who is judge. The notion of heaven contains the idea that the conflicts in us and among us need time to be reconciled. Here lies the idea that we can grow and mature, together and in ourselves.

This is an image which addresses the crippled creation in us and among us, in the fullness of which we can gain new life. If sin is 'rebellion against the creation',[9] then it is grace with body, soul and spirit to open up God's creative forces in us, outside us and among us.

Such a theology starts from a creation in which God saw that all that he had created was good, and which experiences its continuation in the story of Jesus. In the Gospel of Mark (7.37), people see Jesus' healings and are amazed: 'He has done all things well', a repetition of the praise at creation. Therefore for some contemporary theologians the doctrine of original sin no longer has a legitimate place in theology. The Dominican Matthew Fox has proposed replacing original sin with original blessing. He claims that the latter has far more roots in the Bible and can enable people to tackle the tasks of our defective world not as those who are bowed down and corrupted but as friends, as those who are blessed and healed.[10] It is a world which waits for grace, love, renewal and transformation, but the latter can be radiated only if a faith in original goodness is present.

The experience of guilt and the search for forgiveness will largely determine human life. For many situations, forgiveness coming from outside will be life-sustaining. Only forgiveness will also time and again be uncoupled from the church's claim to power. It can be interpersonal forgiveness and also self-for-giveness, which women have already often expressed, i.e. insight into the facts and the liberation of oneself from guilt feelings by means of one's own criteria of value.

It is not a matter of deleting sin from the life of Christians, but of recognizing and identifying the sexism in and among us, and at the same time recognizing the experiences in which we feel ourselves entangled, whether in sickness, guilt, sin, help-lessness and failure or the experiences of salvation and healing, of life-giving forces. Thus an energetic potential could grow which creates space for the experience of numinous forces and intensifies life.

In our culture of guilt with its lack of words for salvation, happiness, forgiveness, we need images which enrich and expand our life and sharpen our senses to disaster and salvation in us and among us.

It is sin to ignore this wholeness. It is grace to open ourselves, body, soul and spirit, to God's friendship in us, among us and outside us.

The following chapter shows how destructive a false under-standing of sin can be and how it can also ruin a relationship of friendship.

6

Jesus' Friend – Mary Magdalene

Yet another tradition of friendship has its roots in the New Testament, but it keeps being forgotten. This is the friendship between Jesus and Mary Magdalene. It is the oldest and most important women's tradition, but was soon suppressed by another women's tradition: Mary the mother of Jesus was favoured by the church as it developed along patriarchal lines. Her role, still thin in the New Testament, was revalued and fantasized on. The result was that in the early period of Christianity, two models of women stood over against each other: that of friendship, embodied by Mary Magdalene, and that of motherhood, depicted in Mary, the mother of Jesus.

While over the years Mary was exalted above all women, Mary Magdalene's descent to become the great sinner began, a role which was equally full of fantasy. In this process it becomes clear that in the structures of the church, which were becoming increasingly powerful, an unmarried mother and friend had inevitably to come off worse than the wife and mother. Here the church made itself a programme which it has maintained down to the present. And the tragic story of Mary Magdalene's friendship began.

As we have to do with a story of massive repression and subtle methods, here once again it needs to be described in full detail.[1] In connection with it we need to ask – with many women today – what form might be taken by a church in the spirit of Mary Magdalene, the first witness to the resurrection, apostle and friend of Jesus.

First let us take a look at the New Testament evidence, beginning with the earlier tradition.

Mary Magdalene's name (Mark 15.40, etc.) primarily indicates her origin. She comes from Magdala on Lake Gennesaret in Galilee. In following Jesus she presumably left her homeland. When the name 'Magdalene' appears, she was probably no longer there. She seems to have been a woman who lived alone, since otherwise her name would have been made more specific with the mention of a male relative. She went from Galilee to Jerusalem with Jesus and the group of disciples from Galilee in company with other women. This discipleship is described with the word 'serve', a word which is used only of women around Jesus. The two other words frequently used in this context, 'follow' and 'go up to Jerusalem', are, as Elisabeth Schüssler Fiorenza remarks, also used of male disciples. The serving, which, as Luise Schottroff points out, means rejecting 'the hierarchical order', links the women disciples to Jesus in a striking way.

Mary Magdalene is always mentioned first in the lists of women which appear in the stories of the passion and resurrection. In parallel to Peter, who is always mentioned first in the group of men, this shows a special authority which she had in the early communities. This authority is mentioned in accordance with the criteria which are given in Acts 1.21f., 25, that of being a 'witness to the resurrection' and apostle.

With the other women she went to the crucifixion, burial and tomb of Jesus, the enemy of the state, and in so doing risked her life. On Easter morning, with them she was given orders to proclaim the message of the resurrection to the male disciples who had run away. John also attributed another special encounter with Jesus to her and, according to Raymond Brown, also regarded her has having taken part in the eucharist, for she heard his voice – a characteristic of the disciples, 'his own', who like the sheep hear the voice of the shepherd. There is mention of 'his own' at the beginning of the last supper.

Mary is not mentioned in Pauline theology, but only the brothers! Is she also included among them, or couldn't Paul accept her (I Corinthians 15.3ff.) as a witness?

In addition, Luke relates her healing from a mental illness (8.3) and says that she belonged to the core of the earliest community in Jerusalem. But there is no mention of a return and temporary stay in Galilee.

Even if the word 'friend' is not yet used of her, she towers above the group of women around Jesus by virtue of a special authority and familiarity with Jesus.

Motherhood versus friendship

Now what do the New Testament reports say about the mother of Jesus?

Mark still brings out in all its sharpness the conflict between mother and son which probably was still based on historical facts; Matthew tones it down by omitting the suspicion on the part of the family that Jesus was crazy (Mark 3.21). Luke waters down the harsh saying of Jesus that only those belong to the eschatological family who do the will of God (Mark 3.35), to the extent of adding to his Gospel stories of the birth and childhood of Jesus which even depict Mary as the obedient maiden who fulfils these requirements (1.38).

However, this picture of the believing, obedient Mary is not then carried through in the Gospel of John: while John – in contrast to the other traditions, which only knew the group around Mary Magdalene – puts her under the cross in order to make her the mother of the Beloved Disciple who is the model of a believing Christian, because of her 'incomplete faith at Cana' she cannot be compared to the Lukan Mary.

So we have a divided New Testament picture of Mary, in which the two main motifs of later mariology, virgin birth and presence under the cross, which have penetrated deep into piety through the artistic depictions of the birth scenes and Pietà, are clearly of later origin. However, the positive evaluation of Mary in Luke and John could not suppress Mary Magdalene. The centre of Christian faith, the resurrection, remained associated with her.

However, already in Luke the tendency to reduce Mary Magdalene's singularity in favour of the group of women can be observed. In Luke, the original tradition, contained above all in Mark, that in contrast to the disciples, who were in love with success, the women were the real disciples of Jesus, and that they knew the messianic secret because they served Jesus, just as he came to serve and to give his life, is joined by a second, which in addition to the obedience and motherliness of the woman also favours the male group of disciples. The alliance of men and motherhood were always stronger than an individual woman.

In the first centuries of church life both models of women could still stand side by side on an equal footing. Mary was one saint among others. But soon, with the Council of Ephesus, the church decided for Mary as *theotokos*, mother of God. Here it took up an image from popular piety and pressed all notions of women into it, and as a result the traditions of friendship were increasingly put on one side. The friends did not find their way into the creed, and Mary Magdalene remained illegitimate.

The momentous distortion of the story of Mary Magdalene and her personality, which extends as far as modern art and literature, began at this time.[2]

How did this fatal falsification of history come about?

Mary's history (Luke 8) was combined with the story of the woman who was a great sinner (Luke 7). Her jar of ointment led her also to be identified with Mary of Bethany, who anointed Jesus (John 12), and in the Western churches, out of three independent female figures there arose a monster and model of sin and grace. This was a development which, as Karl Künstle has pointed out, goes back above all to Augustine: 'As she (Mary Magdalene) once like him lay in the bonds of sin' and had become a comfort to him.[3]

This did not change even with the Reformation, which was again orientated on the Gospels. Luther did not follow the enlightened Faber Stapulensis, who again divided out the three persons of Mary Magdalene, Mary of Bethany and the woman who was a great sinner. For Luther, Mary Magdalene remained the woman who was a sinner, just as according to Calvin's moral ideas, the women disciples of Jesus had been 'calumniated'. The women became models of a new theology of justification, images of sin and grace, without their history, their relationship and their function at the resurrection being discovered. The change to the Roman Breviary in 1978 at least put an official end to the fatal Magdalene tradition.

Btu what does the story of the friend of Jesus look like?

The counter-story

First of all the brief accounts of Mary Magdalene as a close companion of Jesus and the first witness to the resurrection contained in the New Testament once again blossomed with great imagination in the later apocryphal Gospels. What is only hinted at in the New Testament is here worked out fully. Three elements are emphasized: her nearness to Jesus, her special role in the resurrection and her rivalry with Peter.

If a special intimacy between Mary Magdalene and Jesus can be inferred from the New Testament, the Gospel of Philip even speaks of frequent kisses. Mary is regarded as the 'companion' of the Saviour: '. . . the companion of the (Saviour) is Mary Magdalene. (Christ loved) her more than all (the disciples) and kissed her on the (mouth) often. The other disciples were offended at this. They said to him, "Why do you love her more than all of us?" The Saviour answered and said to them, "Why do I not love you like her?"'

According to the Gospel of Mary (Magdalene) she has

insights which are hidden from the other disciples. The erotic fellowship is at the same time a mystical fellowship of the Spirit. In the Dialogue of the Saviour she is not only a visionary who has the full confidence of Jesus but even more: 'a woman who knows the universe'. By comparison with the male apostles, who are regarded as orthodox and who represent the church tradition, she is the Gnostic who places an emphasis on spirit, experience and future. Whereas the men want to hear facts from her, as the witness to the resurrection, she presents a very personal form of the Gospel.

Here the rivalry with the male disciples, which is hinted at in a restrained way in the New Testament, is discussed fully. The Gospel of Mary reports that when the disciples were disheartened and anxious after the crucifixion, they asked Mary (Magdalene) to encourage them by telling them what the Lord had told her in secret. When Peter asked in a fury, 'Did he really speak in secret with a woman (and) not publicly with us? Are we going to change and all obey her? Has he preferred her to us?', Mary, troubled at this outbreak of anger, replied, 'Peter, my brother, what do you think? Do you think that I devised this in my heart or that I am lying about the saviour?' At this point Levi intervenes to mediate in the argument: 'Peter, you have always been impetuous. Now I see you disputing with this woman as with enemies. But if the Saviour has made her worthy, who are you to reject her? Certainly the Lord knew her very well. Therefore he loved her more than us.' Then the others agree in accepting Mary's teachings and go out into the world to preach, encouraged by her words.

There is another dispute between Peter and Mary (Magdalene) in the Pistis Sophia ('Faith and Wisdom'). Peter objects to Mary dominating the conversation with Jesus and displacing the legitimate priority of Peter and his brother apostles. He presses Jesus to order her to be silent and is immediately rebuked. Later, however, Mary concedes to Jesus that she hardly dares to speak freely with him, as – in her words – 'Peter makes me hesitate: I am afraid of him, for he hates the female sex.' Jesus replies that whoever is driven by the Spirit is intended by God to speak, whether man or woman.[4]

Later, there are further traces of the tradition of friendship in the mediaeval legends.[5] In these legends it is striking that the story of the woman who was a sinner is the background against which the story is played out, but that the two other elements of the biblical and also the Gnostic tradition come more markedly into the centre: Mary Magdalene is the closest companion of Jesus, even if she does not kiss his mouth, but his feet. She is called 'friend', an unorthodox expression which is used in mediaeval mysticism. In contrast to the disciples she is the steadfast one, who does not flee and in the encounter with the risen Christ becomes the 'apostle of the apostles'. She is a fascinating preacher, has disciples like her friend and master Jesus, and becomes the missionary saint of France. The pictures of the preaching woman which arise at the periphery of the culture of the woman who was a sinner in the mainstream church depict her in sovereign fashion: in the boat, like her friend Jesus; in the pulpit of a mediaeval cathedral; in parish churches and in market places. Romanesque depictions like those, for example, at the holy sepulchre in the cathedral at Gernrode in the Harz, are particularly impressive: here Mary Magdalene approaches the risen Christ in a majestic attitude, and not kneeling as in later depictions.

After a great effort I found a striking image in Lübeck: on the outside of the wing of an altar triptych, firmly fixed to the wall, Lazarus is kneeling before his sister Magdalene and she makes him bishop of Marseilles. Normally no human eye sees this heretical image, which is an early mockery of the refusal of the priestly ministry to women. I conjecture that in the Celtic-French sphere, which has a long matriarchal tradition, such images of woman could flourish. They again gave space to the original Christian traditions about women.

Recollections of the independent first woman of Christianity then emerge again in the Protestant movements on the periphery of the Reformation churches, but not among the Reformers themselves.

Thanks to the dissemination of the translation of the Bible, women could now read with amazement the real role of Mary Magdalene in the New Testament and identify with her. Katharina Zell, the wife of the Strasbourg reformer, delivered a public funeral oration for her husband and excused herself for this scandal of a woman making a public appearance by saying that she was doing as Mary Magdalene had done. She shyly added, 'with no thought of being an apostle'.

In the next century the Quaker Margaret Fell once more orientated herself self-confidently on the New Testament women, the three Maries, Joanna and Mary Magdalene: 'They handed on the message . . . as the disciples wanted to, but they were not present . . . ' The right of women to speak in the church, which is again reviving, is derived from biblical roots. The Quaker John Rogers calls Mary Magdalene the 'first preacher of the resurrection'.

Later, in the eighteenth century, in the USA the black Methodist Javan Lee derived the right of women to preach from the central Christian message which had been delivered by a woman. In the denominational churches of the USA the voices of women claiming the right to preach keep referring back to Mary Magdalene.

However, it is striking that in the Protestant debate on ordination, at the beginning of this century there was hardly any reference to this first preacher. Perhaps the women concerned had relied on the Pauline vision and version current in the male-dominated church, according to which there is no mention of a woman witness to the resurrection. Certainly Mary Magdalene is mentioned in the Vatican Declaration of 1976, but her role is immediately played down again with the argument that the women were only to prepare the apostles to become the official witnesses to the resurrection.

What the Latin church fathers wanted to achieve with the invention of the figure of Mary Magdalene, namely to prescribe a way of life between desire and killing the flesh, between fornication and holiness, between sin and grace, was inevitably doomed to failure. At the latest since the Renaissance, artists had detached themselves from the 'sinful woman' of church thinking, but they discovered Mary Magdalene as an object of sexual pleasure, as a sex model. She was an attractive, capricious or gentle model, depending on the male needs of the time. At the latest from the time of the Renaissance, the despicable sinner and prostitute had also been made the seductive courtesan depicted by Titian, the loose companion which Shalom Ben Chorin saw in her, or the gentle groupie of the rock opera *Jesus Christ Superstar*, who with her companions and consolation that all was well compensated for the rough world.

However, all this did succeed in ruining the image of the independent first woman of Christianity. What remained beyond the church walls was the recollection of a 'half-crazy woman' who thought that she had seen the risen Christ, mocked by David Friedrich Strauss, or the tender and devoted woman who has been expected everywhere today from Heinrich Böll to Ernst Eggimann:

Jesus
I imagine you loved
mary magdalene
who was beautiful
and smelled of flowers
when you embraced her
her devotion was
so great
like a divine love
I imagine this night
outside history
which overcame all morality

redeem us
jesus
from the Christian sins
make us free

ernst eggimann[6]

However, that is a new day-dream and it is not the whole of the biblical Magdalene. How can she rise again, this friend of Jesus, who makes us God's friends, the apostle of all apostles, who proclaims anew the newness and immediacy of God?

The church in the spirit of Mary Magdalene

Thirty years ago now, Heinrich Böll asked, in view of the 'dryness of the utterly unattractive offer by the church', what a theology of Mary Magdalene, a theology of tenderness, might look like. After all, Jesus touched people, stroked them, kissed them and applied spittle to them, and for him those were means of communication.[7]

Today, confronted with a rigid Petrine church, women are asking what a church in the spirit of Mary Magdalene would look like, a church which is going forwards, which is not fortified and is ready to change.

I imagine three characteristics of such a church:

1. It is moved by the message of the resurrection which is put in the heart, hands and head of a woman, and which this woman, together with many other women, hands on.
2. Her message is closeness to God, and not the distance from God which arose out of the guilt-feelings of the disciples who had left their friend in the lurch.
3. Its social form is not the model of the family with the *paterfamilias*, but the model of the life of the woman who is quite different, who is governed by Eros and friendship.

I shall comment on these three characteristics in turn.

1. Then as now the message of the resurrection is: be as you are, and you will release transforming powers in the world. Mary Magdalene's experience of the resurrection is an example of this. She hears the terrifying statement which has apparently put an end to all friendship, 'Do not touch me!' It is often related to the unearthly light-figure of the resurrection body. But since the risen Jesus wants to be touched by Thomas, this interpretation is unconvincing. Rather, the statement refers to a new kind of relationship between Jesus and Mary Magdalene. It presupposes that they have touched each other before, and that there is an end to this kind of communication. The Risen Christ shows her a changed, independent, free position which she must now adopt towards him, and which has to do with her experience of the resurrection: the message of a life beyond all experiences of death has been put in her heart, her hands, her head, her senses, and this she must now pass on independently. She must introduce it into life, into life in which the ever new life must flow and which never ceases to change. She must now touch life and the future herself, with body and spirit, experience and knowledge, but touching in friendship has equipped her for that.

Such a resurrection scene, which depicts her as independent, can be observed in Gernrode at the holy sepulchre. There the proud figure of Mary comes to meet the Risen Jesus. She does not think of kneeling humbly, in the pose portrayed by almost all the later Easter encounters. Her self-confidence is further illustrated by the gestures she is making with her hands. With her right hand she is touching herself protectively. With her left she is opening herself to the one opposite her. She thus shows an authority which draws on its own creativity and at the same time is open to others.

What powers have been attributed to her emerge from a legend told by a nun from the convent attached to the Magdalene Church in Jerusalem.

When Mary Magdalene meets the risen Jesus and rushes to

tell the disciples, she meets Pontius Pilate and tells him of the Easter miracle. 'Prove it,' he says to her. That same moment a woman comes along with a basket of eggs. Mary Magdalene picks up an egg, and immediately the white egg becomes bright red.

In the Magdalene Church in Jerusalem the egg – symbol of new life and feminine fertility, which is always associated with Astarte, goddess of the spring – is in the hand of Mary Magdalene. It symbolizes a fertility which is not bound up with biological motherhood but releases powers of transformation in the world.

The vision which this produces for us is that in the churches, the powers of transformation and renewal which are hidden and suppressed in women must be addressed and liberated, and that women have a special message for life as it is lived, which no priest, no man, no pope, no state can take from them. There must be women followers of the first woman apostle whose lives are set free for the message of life.

And just as in the group of women around Mary Magdalene, around such women there must also be women who reinforce and strengthen these women – along the lines of the *Affida-mento* of the women of Milan.[9]

2. In Western, Roman theology the basic human experience is guilt and separation from God. It seems to me that already in the story of Jesus, men and women had different experiences which also led to a different experience of guilt. When the disciples fled on the arrest of Jesus, this experience of guilt stamped their relationship to Jesus. Similarly, Paul's theology is influenced by the experience of guilt at having persecuted Jesus. By contrast, the women had other experiences: they were constantly near to him, even under the cross, which for them meant the risk of arrest and death. Nor did they leave the dead and buried Jesus. Closeness, love, being there for one another, stamped their relationship to Jesus. And Mary Magdalene as an

individual and leader of the group of women is an example of this other attitude, which is depicted as companionship, later even as intimacy; it includes kisses on the mouth and tenderness, so that she is called the friend of Jesus who preaches with 'sweet words'.

Here we have to do with different experiences of God from those that have stamped our theology and the church, which are unfortunately experiences only of sin and distance. The experience of closeness has been reserved for mystical and psycho-social theology, which hardly had any influence on the prevailing culture of the church. However, the domination of this theology of distance has two tragic consequences from which we are still suffering today.

First, sin as a fundamental rebellion against God has shifted into sexuality and the human body, a development encouraged above all by Augustine. For him, the desires and drives under which he suffered severely in his youth became the centre and expression of opposition to God. A theology which dominates the body and is hostile to the body, and which can still be found n the doctrine of original sin, was the consequence. Today it is only slowly being countered.

Secondly, the human body became an expression of control over people, a task which the church took over all too readily. It is no coincidence that Augustine described those members which have erections in terms of political rebellion. The church became the instrument of power for the control of sin and the forgiveness of sin. One had to be obedient to her, just as the flesh also had to be obedient to the spirit.

With this concept of sin the church had created for itself a monopoly of power which it is still attempting to maintain today. Here men and women are kept under control, body and spirit, and are called to obedience, rather than to becoming responsible for themselves.

Today women are attempting to start again at this point and to work out the history of discrimination against their bodies, to understand anew the incarnation of God in female flesh and once again to give sexuality an important place in our human life together.

The figure and history of Mary Magdalene stand for such an image of human beings, in which there are no divisions in a close relationship to God. With her people can return to their creative powers and make the church arise again. However, this church will not be supported by obedient men and women, but by men and women who have come of age, who are responsible for themselves and their bodies.

Mary Magdalene as a social symbol

3. What will be the social form of a church which understands itself in terms of a woman who lives alone and does not understand itself in terms of patriarchal family structures? What contours could the church take on here?

Behind our traditional church stand the contours of the family model, shaped by Roman legal thinking. The supreme head is a *paterfamilias*, a man, the pope, the father. It is a characteristic of this family model that the father of the family has power, that the members of the family are subordinate to him and are meant to be obedient. It is also important that another, exclusive, private love is dominant in it. Anyone who lives outside this family without being subject and obedient to it is a heretic. The family community is stamped by the same rituals, hierarchical structures and the cultivation of intimacies, all of which create a feeling of home.

Mary Magdalene cannot represent such a family model.

If we look in the New Testament, it becomes clear that the beginnings of the Jesus movement, especially as they are narrated in the Gospel of Mark, do not know a patriarchal model of the family, but rather an anti-family model as a new community.

According to Mark 10.29f., Jesus promises to all who follow him that they will leave father, mother, wife, children, house, fields, brothers and sisters and will find all this again. However, there will be no father, and there will not be just one house, but houses in the plural. The fellowship which the early Jesus community envisaged is a fellowship of women and men, brothers and sisters, without the domination of a father and without a fixed house in which all live together under one roof. This early statement was an affront to the family model with its patriarchal form, but it could not be maintained. Mark's statement is already watered down in Matthew and Luke.

We rediscover traces of the early models of equality in the further history of Christianity. Here Mary Magdalene also plays a leading role in the Gnostic groups as one who knows, as Wisdom, as a Gnostic. And in the Middle Ages too she reappears at the centre of piety in the Cathar movement, which was built on justice and equality, replacing the Mary of the mainstream church. As the Cathar expert Gottfried Koch emphasizes, this Mary has hardly anything to do with 'the acknowledgment of the equal role of women'.[10] The historian Shulamith Shahar makes a similar remark about the mediaeval women's movement.[11]

If Mary Magdalene is of no use for a patriarchal symbolism, she cannot be commandeered for a mother-centred form of life either. The image of the great mother or the notion of motherhood can hardly be reconstructed from her later history in piety. To my knowledge, the epithet 'mother', which also is applied to the biblical Martha, does not appear for her anywhere. She constantly remains the other woman, the nonmother, the beloved, the friend, the beautiful woman with the loose hair, the dangerous woman who is governed by Eros and not by Caritas. She is disorderly, evading the normal roles and obligations of women, and the danger which she posed was banished by making her a sinner.

So precisely for this reason I would want to begin with her

otherness and see in this her significance for us and our time. I would also want to regard this otherness as a challenge for a church for which unity and affinity play such a central role that it fears diversity and otherness, and brands as heresy all that is 'other'.

Initially, 'otherness' causes fear. We do not want to be different from the others, even if in fact we are. We want to be like everyone else. Women in particular have experienced their otherness in a long painful process. They have come to recognize that they have a different history, different experiences and different knowledge from that of the dominant culture. But at the same time these painful insights also release creative forces by leading us away from well-trodden ways and into new unknown territory. They can make us curious and capable of discovering the other as other. They give us courage to be ourselves.

For Christina Thürmer-Rohr, there is an opportunity for women specifically in the recognition that human beings are different and must not think that they are the same.[12] This extends private and family love into a love of the world which shows itself in a concern for a world inhabited by diverse people. Here in encounters with those who are other and different we find in a new way a development which calls for respect, openness, curiosity about the other, a capacity to listen, attentiveness to detail, doubt about any judgment that could be a prejudice and scepticism about the usual agendas. No one can presuppose any longer that they know and have understood the other. According to Thürmer-Rohr this is an abdication of the position of domination and the certainty of rule and an attempt to practise abdicating rule. Only in this way do we arrive at a political plurality into which each individual is incorporated.

For the philosopher Emanuel Levinas, the face of our time is 'the face of the other'.

Transferred to the church, this would mean an abdication of any totalitarian thought and action and what Sallie McFague sees as a transition to a 'planetary way of thinking' (see p. 20 above). But the others are not only women. There are also the countless unheard voices of the cultures which are not dominant: we meet them in liberation theologies; they do not come to us along what David Tracy has called the asphalt highway of modern rationality.[13] God's voice can be heard again in such other experiences and revelations.

This orientation on the other ultimately has very deep roots in the Christian-Jewish tradition and the recollection of being in the alien land of Egypt: 'Love the stranger. He is like you.' It is the basis of love of enemy and of neighbour in the New Testament, and it is also based on friendship with God.

Mary Magdalene's otherness could take a church back to the roots of its existence. It could lead from disembodied togetherness to embodied communication. It could put listening before speaking. It could again counter the Logos with wisdom. It could bring the Spirit back to earth. It could also make brothers and sisters into friends. In it diversity could be experienced instead of unity, and difference in equality. And a friendship could arise, as in the friendship between Jesus and Mary Magdalene, in which rather than dependence, caring and Eros flourish.

7

Friendly Contacts: Tenderness and Eros

Two ideas have broken into our middle-class and church notions of order in recent decades and have changed and challenged them. They are denoted by the words 'tenderness' and 'Eros', both bound up at an early stage with the figure and history of Mary Magdalene, the friend of Jesus. At first they seem familiar to us. With tenderness we associate closeness, warmth, snuggling up; Eros makes most people think of sexuality. But if we investigate the way in which the words tenderness and Eros have been used in the last thirty years, we make a surprising discovery: tenderness and Eros infiltrate what we commonly call 'love'. They attack a bourgeois love which has been taken over by the church and interpret 'love' with what seem to be highly subjective ideas coming close to sexuality. They refer back to primal states of love and criticize an apparently whole Christian world and a complacent, stable church, in which a hierarchy has repressed the initial equality in Christianity, and later 'love patriarchalism' has suppressed the equality of women and men. Since then tenderness and Eros have found a place – however modest – in our terminology, even if they still often shock people, and they contribute towards opening up new free spaces in our language and thought which have been dominated by thoughts of rule and domination. They are attempts at friendly contacts in the face of growing indifference, which opened up a new culture of relationship, and which were related to both the private and the public spheres. For me, they are the stormy first steps on the way to a culture of friendship.

Tenderness and Eros are not theological concepts. We do not find them in any dogmatics nor directly in the Bible, nor do we probably ever find them in a sermon. But they have a common theological concern: they are meant to revive something of the primal love on this earth and in these conditions. They block any evasion and flight into the beyond. They compel us to take note of an unfriendly and cold world which is falling apart at the seams, and at the same time not to give up the dream of a healing, juster world, a life which begins here and which we can trust and adopt.

Gentle though they may sound, they inexorably attack injustices and have become subversive forces. Tenderness has been called the 'anarchist'. I would call Eros the 'revolutionary'. Are these dangerous lapses into left-wing illusions in our Christianity which is becoming unpolitical? Or are they ideas which we can use for changes which are necessary?

I want to make clear the place there is in our lives for tenderness the anarchist and Eros the revolutionary, and ask what both can offer us, and our situation in life and work.

What is tenderness?

Our linguistic sense makes us feel that tenderness belongs in the feminine sphere. One expects the mother to be tender to her child and the wife to be tender to her husband: 'Zuleika was so tender . . .' At first sight this notion has nothing to do with masculinity.

For Sigmund Freud, who still communicates the feelings of many of our contemporaries about life and sex, tenderness was more of a derailment of the sexual drive, and that was what was important for him. Tenderness was an eroticism diverted from the goal of the sexual drive. Thus for him stirrings of the senses part company with tenderness, and this could be seen as the cause of sexual disturbances.[1]

Nowadays we see this perspective as androcentric. In this case it starts from an understanding of sexuality fixated on the genital area, but one which for many women today is too one-dimensional, which puts intercourse at the centre and does not grasp the women's needs. But feminine sexuality includes tenderness. So Freud's definition is dated and does not yet embrace women's perspective.

Erich Fromm came closer to a definition of tenderness which is valid today in his *Art of Loving*.[2] He rejected the explanation of tenderness as a sublimation of the sexual drive, as Freud understood it. Instead, for him tenderness is the direct expression of love of neighbour, which occurs both in bodily and in non-bodily form. For him tenderness is 'without greed'. Here Fromm had broken away from a narrowly conceived understanding of sexuality and had given tenderness a place in human social life.

But tenderness, which had so been belittled, which had been seen as feminine and had been shunned, exploded in 1969 when Heinrich Böll wanted it to be the motive force for a church which was anything but tender. 'People want to communicate!', he began. 'Just imagine that: people want to communicate.' And he continued:

> Too much is withheld from Christians, including the sexual and erotic tendernesses which are 'allowed' and 'not allowed'. I cannot imagine how things look in the consciousness of those who cheerfully call on people to have children and at the same time are not clear that the procreation of a child is quite impossible without the sexual excitement at least of the male. I know, people don't talk about it, but in that case they shouldn't talk either about love, marriage or family. They shouldn't even get involved in them. But at any rate Christ touched people, stroked them, kissed them, smeared them

with spittle: he brought wholeness and healing. Kissing, stroking, touching, spittle were means of communication for him. Who can be surprised that in view of the 'dryness', the utterly untender offer of the church, people arrive at the most crazy and sometimes perverse ideas? I don't know whether they ever find it, but what they are looking for and what they want to give is joy . . .[3]

In the face of a desiccated theology with its unsensual language he called for a theology of Mary Magdalene, a theology of tenderness. Here tenderness had found its place as communication through the senses in a culture of church and society which isolates people and is remote from the senses, a place which it has kept down to the present day. A society, a church, stamped with fears about contact was called on to communicate differently, through the senses, through the body. Activities which had previously not been addressed or had belonged merely in a private intimate realm like kissing, caressing, touching, became open to a new interpersonal way of relating to one another. This was not the old 'Be nice to one another . . . ' This was a new culture which broke open the traditional closedness. In his problem case Böll began with the Catholic church, but it soon proved that the Protestant church and our whole social culture were equally affected.

In retrospect I would want to call this discovery and this significance of tenderness a cultural shift in which the old Western split between body and spirit was to be attacked and done away with. Böll rediscovered the human body as the only meaningful and sensual field of action in our relationships and tenderness not only as a feminine property, but as a basic human need which liberates us from being closed in and closed off. The Western dualism which goes against the Hebraic notions of totality in the Jesus movement and early Christianity had found its way into theology with the assimilation of Christianity to a social, Roman-Greek pattern of thought. It had shaped the churches and cultural thought and produced our culture of domination and rule which are hostile to the body. Böll suddenly saw the body once more as a place of healing and as the centre of salvation, and he discovered the disembodied God, the church's God without a body, who had become a victim of the rationalistic Christianity of the Enlightenment. His speech in Stockholm on receiving the Nobel Prize was a plea for this forgotten, embodied God, to whom the incarnation of the human corresponded and who precisely because of his embodiment also hallows all the elements.[4] The roll at breakfast can then be interpreted sacramentally; the cup of tea can become the holy chalice. Böll discovered the meaning of the incarnation in an ardent plea for the re-sacralizing of the banal and the trivial.

But the bodies which are shut in and shut off can come to life again only through touch, through contact. Tenderness takes place through touch. Tenderness is a notion which occurs today in psychosomatics, ecology and feminist theology, and we must continually become aware of its extreme importance. Touching is a somatic gesture of healing. 'I touch, and therefore I am touched,' is a motto in ecology. 'Becoming human through touching' is the way in which Hildegund Keul describes friendship. Touching touches our anxieties about contact, our cool detachment in society, our stuffy attitude in the church pews, our 'tastelessness' at the eucharist. Touching makes us experience our bodies again and finally also accept them, love them; it makes us see them again and learn to listen to them. Our bodies, which – as Norbert Elias has shown – have become alien and hostile in a process of ongoing civilization! Our body is stimulated in touching through our skin, our largest and most sensitive organ, and this makes it possible for us to experience again the totality of body, soul and spirit. According to Böll, tenderness is also healing. Just as Jesus healed with his tender touch and not so much by great words, so too men and women can heal and be made whole. This healthily puts in question our whole church culture and tradition of using words. As a consequence of this, the metaphor 'ladder of tenderness' immediately appeared in the text of the 1971–1975 Würzburg synod.[5]

Political tenderness

In 1979, in his book _Tenderness and Pain_, Kurt Marti gave tenderness yet another special emphasis, a political one.

> Tenderness is equally sensuality, which makes people intelligent, like intelligence, which makes them sensual. Even its intoxication does not deaden but illuminates. The anarchist will be able to rule only where there is no longer any rule. Her pathos is that of the inconspicuous: a helpless gesture, a flash of lightning or a shadow in the other perspective, a spontaneous movement which suddenly becomes the cornerstone and hinge of all being now and there.[6]

In Marti's tenderness, sensuality is now joined by intelligence, insight into reality. There is no intoxication, no diffuse feeling, but light and clarity or, as he is fond of saying, precision. 'Tender and precise' is a favourite combination of words for him and indicates his concern: for a new, critical, revolutionary perspective which sees the human reality beyond the dominant power structures and wants to do justice to them. In this way God's righteousness becomes visible. Tenderness as an anarchist becomes necessary in order to disempower the unjust situations of power, the claims to power, the expressions of power. Where God is proclaimed as someone who is in power in this way there is no tenderness, and tenderness will never be able to arise between rulers and ruled. By contrast, tenderness discloses the banality, the triviality; it is the everyday miracle. As with Böll, the everyday, the banal, is hallowed. Tenderness transforms our reality. The _homo faber_ becomes the _homo admirans_. Wonderment enters the world where everything seemed manipulable. For those who wonder, the earth is again holy, and creation faith is a faith in the quality of matter. However, no victorious world-view is bound up with such amazement. Tenderness makes people vulnerable. It is 'a helpless gesture, a flash of lightning in another perspective, a spontaneous movement . . .' God can be just as helpless and vulnerable. Marti does not see a Lord God, a powerful Goddess. God is tenderness, love, pain. Tenderness is one of God's daughters and is 'unswervingly subversive'. Tenderness can similarly be called God's incognito. But Marti can also speak of the 'wrath of divine tenderness' which attacks power and injustice.[7]

If for Heinrich Böll it is the dry, uncommunicating churches which are the catalyst for fantasies of tenderness, for Marti it is the theological experiences of power and domination. These disclose to him another level of encounter and experience, a sphere free of domination.

Now there is something striking here: those who are thinking about tenderness are above all men, and since tenderness is associated with feminine modes of behaviour, that is astounding. Granted, increasingly there are also images of tenderness among women. But that seems to derive more from a general cultural trend than from a special need of women.

Men discover tenderness

How has it come about that men and not women have called for and stimulated a theology of tenderness? The reason may be that women are afraid of being forced back again into the niche of tenderness and motherlinesss. Tenderness does not seem for them initially to have proved to be a liberating, renewing, emancipatory force. But where is the context for such a notion if not among them? Are not men miles away from tenderness and perception of the body because of their culture, politics, education and socialization? How did reflections about tenderness arise from their side?

I think that tenderness is an early emancipatory concept from a male movement which did not come about. It is a matter of catching up with the experience which a boy, a man, traditionally could hardly have, if at all, in our society. In a society orientated on the male individual the boy must learn early to detach himself from his mother and from the primal experience of warmth, closeness, security. In this process of disaccustoming himself to these things, he also often learns to repress or even to despise these spheres in order to become a man in a society of male values. 'Tenderness' now represents an attack on hierarchies, power structures and also on fears of contact. This kind of attack was in part reflected in the student revolt of 1968. 'The tenderness of the Kalashnikov' is an apt expression for the lofty claims of a tender justice and the combination of justice, embodiment and violence which did not succeed, eventually coming to grief in the terrorism of the Red Army Faction.

Despite all the absurdities associated with it, I would want to designate tenderness as a rediscovery of the sense of touch which could not come alive in an androcentric culture and a male socialization. It is the highly cautious approach to the body through the skin. It is no coincidence that both thinkers, Böll and Marti, end up in an expectation which is quite unusual in theology, an expectation of the holiness of matter, the embodiment of God, the sacralization of the trivial. With the discovery of tenderness, a decisive, albeit modern step has been taken towards the rediscovery of the body in theology. But above all a first emancipatory step has been taken – away from the feminine spheres which have been abandoned and betrayed. In this trend the educationalist Wolfgang Dietrich has transformed the old educational ideal for boys, 'Thank God for what makes you tough' into 'Thank God for what makes you tender'.[8] Tenderness is not something which traditional masculinity takes for granted. As a man, Herbert Haag thinks that it takes courage. 'We must not shirk it!'

For women, tenderness is not so much something that is hardly forgotten, but something that they must free themselves from, as from the empathetic continuum with the mother. For them it can become something shapeless and soft, which hinders their autonomy and which they have quickly to repress on their way to assimilation to society.

But it is true for everyone, women and men, that tenderness is the recurrent and long-suppressed recollection of the first security given by our mother, by skin contact with her. Tenderness is a reflection back on our origin, on our first experience of our co-humanity. But it is also connected with our helplessness, our exposure and our fragility, in which we have experienced protective power, acceptance and protection through which we could grow and mature. To this degree the tenderness which we have and which we hand on is preserving and healing love, a presence free of desires. But over and above this, women must ask of Heinrich Böll's demand for a theology of Mary Magdalene's tenderness whether here we do not have the projection of a social imperfection, a lack, namely tenderness, back on to women, without women themselves defining what a theology of Mary Magdalene is for them.

What now is the contribution that women can make to a new culture of friendliness? What was their discovery?

What have women put in place of tenderness?

Eroticism as women's power

Just as the word 'tenderness' emerges in the theological and political literature of the 1970s, so the word 'Eros' emerges again in the women's literature of the 1980s. It has a provocative, challenging effect and calls for critical discussion, for traditionally Eros has dangerous connotations – longing, desire, impulsiveness – and in a phase of Protestant theology Eros was also still sharply separated from Agape, true Christian love.

What did women want to express by this? What did Eros represent for their scheme of life? For a friendly world?

One of their most striking representatives, the Afro-American Audre Lord, wrote around 1980:

> We are gradually discovering eroticism by feminine stan-
> dards as something which is not limited to any part of the
> body or even to her body as such; as an energy which is not
> just diffuse but omnipresent, which expresses itself in part in
> joy – bodily, emotional and psychological joy – and in shared
> work . . . Eroticism is a potential, a means of life in all of us,
> which belongs to a deeply feminine and spiritual level and is
> firmly rooted in the power of our unexpressed feelings.[9]

But in a male society eroticism is regarded as a sign of female inferiority, and women have been made to suffer under eroticism and to despise themselves for it. As Audre Lord goes on to say, 'We have been brought up to fear our Yes to ourselves, our deepest longing.' But that need not lead to resignation: 'If we begin to live from within, in contact with the power of eroticism in ourselves, and if we allow ourselves to be inspired to work on our environment from there, then women become responsible for themselves.' So eroticism is developed from the deep defect of women's experience, from their inability to say Yes to themselves in their whole person, from the experience of being nothing, from the knowledge of being quite different. Instead of now seeing themselves as being without a place and a utopia – a comment which can be heard from some feminist theorists – with eroticism a deep love of life is discovered, a germ of vitality which could not be killed and which has not died.

But this orientation on life is now understood in a different way: it is not limited to a part of the body; it is not fixated on the genitals. Nor is it only related to the other, but has a wide effect and makes women responsible for broader areas of life.

If we compare this rediscovery of Eros with the rediscovery of tenderness, it is striking that here we have more than the regaining of a sense of touch, far more. Here once again there is the discovery of a power in life which has been excluded. The failure to perceive it forced women aside and robbed them of their personhood.

Women, Dietmar Mieth remarks, do not need to learn 'the art of being tender'.[10] Instead of this they have to rediscover their buried feelings. They have to begin to feel. They have to feel and again become conscious of their feelings and their longing. As Audre Lord puts it, 'Eroticism is not just a question of what we do, it is a question of the strength or intensity of the feeling when we do it . . . Once we know to what degree we are capable of experiencing satisfaction, intensity, fulfilment, we can also recognize the diverse efforts in our life which bring us nearest to this fulfilment. The goal of all our doing is to shape our life and the lives of our children in a richer, more worthwhile way.' So all our efforts can become a 'celebration of the erotic'.

Along with tenderness, Eros also stands over against an unsatisfied, commercialized world. If tenderness was a protest against what was rigid, dry, rationalistic, against the power-plays, Eros becomes a general protest against a male world in which women are used, defined and robbed of their person-hood. If tenderness already attacked part of such a male world, with Eros it is torn off its hinges. If tenderness was a gentle, non-violent attack, Eros becomes the revolutionary banner in a world in which women now seize the power to define Eros and liberate it from its narrow sexual connotations so that it becomes a primal power of passionate self-knowledge, relation-ship to others and the world. If with tenderness men are redis-covering their abandoned bodies, if they want to savour the world again with a bold step towards tenderness, i.e. repair it, women come up against injuries which cannot simply be repaired. They can be healed only if women abandon this world and begin to shape their own lives. Here we are no longer talking about defects in society. We are talking about seeing its brokenness, which is reflected in women.

Nevertheless, Eros and tenderness have much in common. Both are spontaneous, irrational attacks by love on a world in which love is dead. I see the difference between them as being that women are now standing the pleasure that has been denied them and which has gone bitter on the head, or better on the foot, of reality and declaring that it is the principle of the world. A revolutionary passion orientated on pleasure is arising out of more timid, pleasurable tenderness.

However, the sociologist Christina Thürmer-Rohr shows how little this 'pleasure' has to do with our individualistic, bourgeois-selfish preoccupation with pleasure. For her such erotic pleasure has two dimensions.

First, for her, pleasure in the world in the face of its destruction is important for life, and pleasure in loss is fatal. If erotically, pleasurably, lovingly, we enter into a new relationship with the world and get a new relationship to it, then things and people take on a new quality. In touching and being touched in this way we lose our indifference.

Secondly, this gives rise to a new culture of relationship in which the others are discovered in their life-giving energy. Something has also been 'touched' with tenderness. But here in this relationship which is called Eros, the incarnation of the human first takes place. Eroticism is our longing for mutual association. I need you and I am needed. You need me and you are needed. Incarnation takes place in reciprocity, in mutual giving and taking.

This pleasure is like a bridge to the world and to other people which can be felt with the senses. 'The act of love towards the world is to restore it, to go on it and constantly to prevent its collapse.'[11] Pleasure is a potential in all of us. More than with men, however, with women it is a buried source of power from which change can come.

The chubby Eros of Greek saga, illegitimate but of divine origin, unpredictable and mostly confusing, has again become the primal power that he once was. Eros has become the key for many relationships which are to be defined anew, and it occurs in the most varied spheres. Thus for example Evelyn Fox Keller can suggest using loving, erotic ideas in research instead of exploitative ones. Instead of penetrating the object to be researched (in parallel to male pleasure), subject and object should be seen to be related, a relationship in which there is intimacy and distance, empathy and respect for the other. For her the highest form of love is a love which allows intimacy without doing away with the differences.[12]

Eros in Christianity

Another sphere in which Eros is reappearing is feminist theology. If Böll had already discovered the tender Jesus who heals, touches with spittle, for Marti Jesus was described as a 'phallocrat not fixated on the genitals', around whom there was a fluid of freedom and Eros, then Eros as 'erotic power' once again reverses the relationships.

For the American theologian Rita Nakashima Brock, Jesus can no longer be thought of alone, but only in the community of such erotic power as binds him – above all – to women. He needs people to free him, just as he freed people for the power of Eros. So for Brock the centre of Christianity is no longer the Christ but the 'Christa/Community' (see above p. 38), where this erotic power of mutuality is at work, the power of love which accompanies from the beginning, and which is the fundamental power of being.[13]

Finally, feminist theology not only refuses to deny the opposition of Eros and love and – as happens from the male side – speaks of the love of agape for Eros ('Agape loves Eros!'), but claims that Eros is also defined by Agape.

A book appeared in 1930 which shaped and constrained a whole generation of theologians. It was Anders Nygren's *Agape and Eros*. In it Eros was regarded as self-seeking love, whereas Agape was the authentic Christian love which seeks out the neighbour.[14] But against the biblical background, what we had once learned in Western Christianity now looks quite different.

In his hymn to love (I Corinthians 13.12), Paul says that love never stops. Faith and prophecy remain fragmentary; only in seeing face to face does perfect knowledge come about, is love made reality. But, as Dietmar Mieth points out, this word 'know' still has connotations of the Hebrew term which denotes the mutual knowledge of spouses as a description for the act of love.[15] So both the love of God for humankind and also the relationship of men and women to God is expressed in a term which embraces both eroticism and sex.

The word 'know' (*gignoskein – yada*) also plays an important role in the story of the woman with a flow of blood (Mark 5.29,36), where it expresses the intimate, physical, mysterious event between the woman and Jesus. After she has touched Jesus' garment, it is said of her that she 'felt = knew' in her body that she had been healed of her torment. And at the same time it is said of Jesus that he too 'felt = knew' what had gone out of him. Something mutual has happened in this process of healing, an exchange of erotic energies.

So in New Testament thought, knowledge of God, redemption and healing are still wholly denoted in the language of passion, intimacy and eroticism. The word 'Eros' itself does not occur in the New Testament, but new research has shown that the meaning of Eros is also contained in the New Testament word Agape. Eros and Agape are still closely connected in this way in the sixth century in Maximus Confessor, and the Eros of God can be called the love of God:

The first cause of the heavenly Eros is God, in a way which is boundless and without cause. Now if this Eros really is love and if it is written that God is love, then it is clear that the all-uniting Eros, i.e. love, is God.

And at another point:

In so far as it is Eros and Agape, it moves all that is capable of Agape and Eros to itself. God moves and is moved . . . as seeing, it longs to become; as loving, to be loved.[16]

However, as a result of Augustine, his distrust of the impotent human will and the way in which human beings have succumbed to its drives, in Western theology love was compartmentalized and put in a hierarchical pattern of order. God and human beings were seen as being at a distance, and the passion of eroticism no longer fitted into this relationship with God which still stamped early and Eastern Christianity.

But the love of self and neighbour which Jesus expects in the Gospels can only be understood under the aspect of loving passion, as it is to be found in eroticism. It is a love which is whole and makes whole, which brings together the body and the head, the spheres which have broken apart in our culture, which combines our mind and our senses, and sets in motion our will along with our feelings.

Put in present-day language, love would then mean asking about oneself, one's own wishes and longings, and doing something about them.

Only in desire to we come nearer, do we come near to the other. Eros is a term which needs to be regained for such a curious, passionate concern which penetrates to the depth.

However, a Swiss psychotherapist has asked critically whether there is still enough power in Christianity to revive Eros as an interpersonal, divine force. She points out that the Christian movement which originally arose from the 'impulse of Eros' soon replaced the dynamic interpersonal relationship and flow expressed by Eros, with a 'static, satisfied and controllable relationship', namely Agape. And the truly Christian-Jewish ritual, the eucharist, has been distorted by its negative connotations of guilt, sin and a refusal of love.[17]

Can women also revive Eros in the churches? Will Christian men and women make room for new friendly contacts?

From Eros to housework

But how can women first of all call on these healing energies for their everyday life? What does Eros, this energy which transforms reality, look like in our everyday routine occupations? How, for example, can we discover the Eros of housework?

Traditionally housework has little to do with God, and there is little reflection on it in theology. But it has recently become a topic of feminist theology. Whereas already with Luther the maid with her broom was doing God a service, if one looks a little closer, Luther himself shunned the lowly aspects of housework, changing babies' clothes, the childhood sicknesses, the dirt, and encouraged himself and others to do this in 'the obedience of faith'. There was still no trace of an Eros, a love, of these occupations, which in fact make up life.

That is why in her investigations of housework Ina Praetorius has spoken of 'material spirituality'. By spirituality she means 'the immediate perception of meaning which takes place in the consciousness in the course of a particular activity and which is felt to be wholesome, happy, binding, creating order in a positive sense'. These are experiences which she also knows from classical spiritual exercises.

For her, housework now means something like a ritual for the everyday needs of children, women and men and serves everyday life. Furthermore it is immediately social and is focussed on human life together. Thirdly, it creates order again out of the constant chaos – a wholesome order, even if it can quickly lapse back into an equally wholesome chaos. Fourthly, such work can make necessary activities enjoyable activities, for example in the unspectacular aestheticism of everyday life. And fifthly, it serves to sustain life. Hidden here in the small framework is its significance for the wider framework, politics.

'If housework is shared out fairly, it is no longer the service of the maids to the masters, but the service of all to all, reciprocity.'[18]

For Praetorius, tenderness is another aspect of such a utopia of reciprocity. It denotes a love of little things which come to light again by the 'transformation of the trivial'. I myself see tenderness as being closer to Eros, the passionate love which seeks and discovers. And just as tenderness is called an 'anarchist' who, as Karl Marti points out, emerges where there is no longer any domination, so too Eros creates areas free of domination, in which justice and equality are at home.

If we see housework in terms of this comprehensive picture, the great cosmos of God opens up in our little cosmos, the *oikos*. It is reflected in housework: in setting free the energies which bind everyone together, in the functions which heal our bodies and nourish our spirits, in the creative power which orders chaos and never makes the order a divine principle, in enjoying the aesthetics in the face of the incomplete, in removing and cheerfully enduring the ever-recurring dirt and dust.

Eroticism as a means of life – as Audre Lord understood it – reaches into the forgotten realms which through women are again making a claim to being the meaning and realization of justice.

The rediscovery of tenderness and Eros are sometimes pathetic-seeming attempts to revive the old Christian love and replace rigid structures with friendly contacts. Different as they both are, and different as their settings are, in their passion for life they nevertheless become one in the following points.

With them powers of life which have been buried are rediscovered, and through them we experience that the head/spirit no longer dominates the body, that the senses need no longer disappear and that the body returns.

Now people are no longer isolated individuals but are related to others. Through touching and being touched by these others, healing and incarnation takes place.

The little things, the banal, the trivial are also healed by attentiveness, tenderness, precision, and in this way justice comes about.

The healing of the brokenness, dryness and comfortlessness

of this world is not shifted into another world, but takes place here in the pleasure with which we turn to the world and change it with our mutual energies.

Tenderness and Eros are possibilities of approaching oneself, others and the world afresh. It is a way on which we are hurt, but it is a way against hardening and being torn apart and an attempt at healing and friendship.

8

My Body – My Friend

However, there is not just friendship between persons; there is also, as the Brazilian liberation theologian Rubem Alves writes, a 'friendship between human being and thing, human being and animal, human being and plant'.[1] Others who have thought and written about friendship like Sallie McFague and Carter Heyward have already made similar observations. Those who feel in friendship with God that they are free and untroubled also experience a new friendly relationship to their own environment. I think that one important relationship of friendship in this area which so far has hardly been singled out as a topic is friendship with one's own body. In the history of Western Christianity the body has been regarded more as an enemy than as a friend. God and body could not be thought of together, and Paul's deep sigh, 'Nothing good dwells in my flesh', brought in its train a long tragic history of hatred and mistrust of the body. And indeed those who see on our earth the bodies destroyed by war, sickness and catastrophe, and perceive the violence, the hatred and the brutality which slumber in people and do not cease to break out, will have to agree with the apostle. Human bodies with their desires and drives, human bodies as scenes of destruction, are terrifying, and make many people prefer to escape into the apparently untouchable real of the spirit or the soul.

But the Christian tradition also speaks another language: God has become human, and the fact that God has taken a body requires us to ask again about our bodies and their share

in the divine. There are no laments about the unreliable body in
the Gospels. On the contrary, the Gospels are to be read as a
fascinating history of the body, in which the sick, disheartened,
destroyed body delivered over to death is healed, raised up,
encouraged and restored to life. 'Which is it easier to say?' Jesus
asks his opponents, '"Your sins are forgiven" or "Get up and
walk"?' And he himself gives the answer by telling the sick man,
'Pick up your bed and walk.' Our church culture, which is concentrated on sin and forgiveness, should reflect on the way in
which it still ignores the human body.

If today we are to reflect again on the meaning of becoming
bodies, then we can do so only if we discover the history of the
contempt for women's bodies which slumbers equally deeply in
the Christian tradition, read it again and begin once again from
here to see God and the body together. That means that we
must ask about our relationship to our bodies, about Paul's fear
of the body and the hatred of the body which since Augustine
and his doctrine of the drives has tormented Christianity. It
turned into a fatal mistrust of the body, and we must replace it
with a new way of dealing with our own bodies, which I would
want to term friendship. And just as trust comes first in any
friendship, so too trust in our own bodies will be the important
step we need to take towards such a friendly relationship which
is not determined by exploitation, indifference and anxiety.

When I look round at feminist theology, however, I am
struck by how little expression has so far been given to such
friendship. So far feminist theology has expended little faith,
hope and love on our bodies. Rather, we are warned against
rejoicing in our bodily nature. There is constantly a fear of
lapsing into feminine notions of the body, notions which are
misunderstood biologically. Here the notion of wholeness is
mistrusted, although it is never intended statically but always
dynamically. Here there is an anxious concern that our desire
for aggression is diminishing and that we are prematurely enter-
ing a wholesome world of the body. Only in the visions of a

woman church, where wounds are bound and salvation is celebrated, or in the utopias of a new society and its collective body,
do women risk a look at another world. But how will I succeed
in healing the splits within myself?

Things seem to me to look better among the religious feminists who have shaken off Christian theological thinking about
sin and conflict, and who like the American Starhawk can say
unconcernedly that the image of the Goddess teaches women to
see themselves as divine, their aggressions as healthy and their
bodies as holy.[2]

New knowledge of the body

Women doctors in particular show how difficult it is to get
away from fear of the body and alienation from the body. For
one of the issues is our own mistrust of and lack of confidence
in the body, and the fact that we seem to be delivered up to
the medical technological developments in our society. Many
people, above all women, have become accustomed to looking
at their own organs with disapproval or to controlling them
and seeing them as an enemy of their own lives and plans.
Health magazines and the media, with a wealth of information,
have often had not so much the effect of enlightening people as
of making them insecure and prompting them to anxious self-
examination and the fear of sickness. It would be healthier to
get to know our bodies better, to experience their tensions,
weaknesses and energies, and to regain a sense of them. Just as
in any friendship only reciprocity creates a living relationship,
so we need to perceive the language of our own body, to note its
signals and to take them seriously, though of course these can
be different in every phase of life. Otherwise the body can be
provoked and react with illnesses. But new attention can give
rise to a trust in oneself and the body.[3] On the basis of this the
doctor Ingrid Olbricht can say, 'My body – my friend'.

More serious and even more difficult to penetrate are the

modern practices which are offered by medicine and are apparently indispensable for health. Women above all are dependent
on them through their life-cycles of pregnancy, birth and
menopause. Consequently in 1991 Barbara Duden, a historian
of medicine, declared that a woman's body was a public place.
It is inspected by representatives of all the sciences – lawyers,
doctors, theologians – the child is really detached and isolated
from it, and the person and dignity of the woman's body no
longer has a role. In 1997 Duden said that striving for health
was a 'pathogenic enterprise' and that women's need for health
today was disempowering them.[4] The modern woman, she
says, has become a risk, a risk which is countered by all the
medical techniques available. As a result the woman's body has
become a technogenic body based on medicine, delivered over
the delusion that health can be made. It is often no longer
possible to think of the well-being of a concrete tangible body.
and contact with the doctor often brings more confusion and
anxiety than encouragement.

In contrast to a mechanistic understanding of health of the
kind also advocated by the World Health Organization, namely
that being healthy means being free from diseases, Duden
argues that the *ars patiendi*, the art of suffering, should be
learned. This is not a retreat into the mysticism of suffering and
masochism, a renunciation of doctors and medicine; it means
becoming aware of the mobility and liveliness of what happens
in the body. For me that means experiencing a friendship with
my body which flourishes in the ups and downs, in closeness
and distance, in pain and pleasure.

On the way to being my own body I also find helpful the discovery of spiritual capacities of the body, for example the
notion that we 'understand with the body'. This expression
comes from Christa Wolf, who is presumably influenced by the
American writer Adrienne Rich.[5] Here another dimension of
the body is addressed, with which we are barely familiar and
which we should similarly approach with reverence. We think

that we can solve the problems of our own and public life with a rational logic, without needing feelings, senses. But is precisely through feelings and senses that we most often get a better approach to reality. Our body is a thinking, remembering, foreseeing organ which can make people shrewd and wise and make a 'multi-value logic' possible.[6]

As early as 1981 the American feminist theology Beverly Wildung Harrison started the attempt in moral theology to think through the body. Harrison's basis was Rosemary Ruether's research into the baneful dualism of body and spirit and the negative assessments of the woman which were connected with it. She discovered a disembodied rationality in male theological thinking and called on feminists to begin with our body, our self. In the end all knowledge is knowledge mediated by the body, which is rooted in our sensual perception. But this communicates to us the way in which we are bound up with the world. 'Unless we live deep in our body, in our self, the possibility of moral relationships between us is also destroyed.'[7]

What, for example, would a feminist theology of the body look like which begins with the body, disempowers all pale conceptuality and is based on reality? What magic could we develop in ourselves and among ourselves if we learned again to detect and see Spirit in the body in us and among us?

Freeing oneself from false attributes

How do we get out of our long Western, Enlightenment tradition, which is so split and which splits us? How do I succeed in respecting my own bodily nature in friendship with my body, or even in discovering the sacred materiality of my body?

First of all I must make it clear to myself that the friendly way to healing the body is a process of the same kind as our healing of divisions and splits (see above, p. 7). Particularly in connection with women, Anne Wilson Schaef has observed that healing is a process which begins in the sick persons themselves.[8]

For men, on the other hand, healing usually takes place from outside and happens beyond their persons. So wholeness and healing presuppose my co-operation. There is also stagnation or regression in a process. Any linear haste goes against a living process. The incorporation of failure and laziness, which have a prime place in the church's catalogue of sins, is also indispensable.

One important step on such a way is to become conscious of false prescriptions for what bodies should be like. These prescriptions vary widely: there is the power of fashion which compels us to be fat, thin, pale or brown, which makes us feel good in garments which cling to the skin or loose robes. But what does *me* good?

There are also the medical prescriptions already mentioned above, which persuade women into an unreliable body that diverges from the norm and which have strengthened women in their social attitude of humility. There are also the cultural prescriptions which govern us. To the present day, we are surrounded by the culture of an almighty phallus which towers high into many psychotherapeutic practices, while the significance of the woman's distinctive sexual organ, the clitoris, is not known and women are unaware of their own sexual organ and their own sexual needs. And finally, we constantly prescribe to ourselves how we should be: skilled, perfect, efficient, and at the same time with a keen ear for others. For many women squaring the circle, the impossibility of the possible, has almost become a model. But am I something that can be torn apart in different directions? The body has been muted, the senses function only in a direction which has been learned, and no notice is taken of dreams any more. To recognize my own voice again, after it has been distorted by others, is perhaps the most complicated act in this process of becoming whole.

Healing self-insight

Still, for anyone who succeeds in pushing aside the grey veil of alien prescriptions and their own determination by others, a broad new territory opens up. Instead of a pernicious determination by others they can expect friendship and healing insight into themselves. Given what has been neglected, this can be painful. But what can really open up to us is a miracle of new creation: the miracle that can be seen in me and my body when the slumbering talents, the energies which have never been set in motion, come to the fore. I am my body. My body is not a rigid housing but a field of energy of tremendous extent. My body is my friend, in which I can live in friendship with all that is in it, with all that makes me afraid and all that give me pleasure.

In such processes many women experience their bodies as totalities, no longer split into feeling and mind, the body no longer deprived of its head or the head of its body. The 'illegitimate' spheres of our person – illegitimate because they are irrational – again become valuable. Some women discover that their own sexual wishes, which are fulfilled not just in intercourse but in a total grasp of the other, may legitimately be fulfilled. Others experience the happiness of feeling as they think and thinking as they feel. For some the apparent triviality of their experiences at home and in everyday life are now the source of their own judgment. They discover that housework, this often unpopular physical work, is work which creates meaning and banishes chaos in creation, which can become the experience of a 'material spirituality'[9] (see above, p. 100).

The senses, too, belong in this cosmic dance in which I learn to move. Not the senses which have always been attributed to women, the sense of comfort and the comfortable, but rather a sense of oneself, which has been taken away early from children, above all from women. By now our sense organs have become one-dimensional: we hear with our ears and obey. But we are learning to hear again our own voice and the many soft voices in our world. Our eyes are focussed on objects, but we have seldom practised looking inwards and seeing the invisible. Yet our senses are capable of perceiving things that we have not heard or seen. Through them our body becomes a little cosmos full of experiences and knowledge, a creative place.

Nelle Morton, one of the first feminist theologians, has even spoken of a fruitful chaos in us, when our senses whirl and something of totality is detected. 'We learn to listen with the whole body, to hear with the eye, to see with the ear and to speak with the hearing, because we know that the spirit is present in a way which is static and not dynamic.'[10]

The experience of totality in ecstasy, in prayer, in rapture has always been an expression of supreme religious feeling. Now women are experiencing in many thousands of everyday experiences that their bodies are places of wholeness and healing. Totality has returned to earth, has acquired feet and hands, is earthed.

Natality and curiosity

If we learn to see women's bodies as places of a healing relationship, we must lastly look again at the entry of our body into the world, our birth. In Christianity birth has always stood in the shadow of rebirth and baptism. It long bore the stigma of uncleanness. Natality – our being born – was always less important than mortality. Western philosophy and theology ranged itself around mortality, above all fixated on cross and death. The philosophers Hannah Arendt and Annegret Stopczyk[11] have again given natality a central place in their thought and have directed our gaze to the miracle of our early body. Instead of being fixated on the linear and unavoidable outcome of our life in death, we can orientate ourselves on our being born as a pleasure in new beginnings and a surprise which is never lost.

'Unto us a child is born' is the foundation Hannah Arendt gives to this perspective. We too are born; we do not become children of God and friends of God only through the purification of baptism – as some churches still see it today – but through being born, being created. Thinking in terms of friendship removes the barriers which we have put up to bar direct access to God and the divine.

As I see it, a deep and fine curiosity of life lies hidden in our being born, in our bodies. Thürmer-Rohr thinks that this curiosity is necessary for our encounter with others (p. 83). Curiosity has something quite animal about it. It motivates the smallest children, their capacities and their desire to discover what is around them; it awakens the senses and sets the members in motion. In the Christian anthropology contaminated by Augustine it was part of the evil greed, the seeking and drive which had to dominate human beings. But for me curiosity is one of the hardly conscious capacities which are implanted into our bodies at birth. Curiosity is love, the Eros for the new, for transformation, for being other, for the culture. It can be directed into the wrong channels, but it remains an independent creative bodily energy which goes beyond our rational reason, and we can be surprised at its positive powers. After a time of mourning following the death of her husband, the poet Marie-Luise Kaschnitz described her return to life as the return of her curiosity:

> My curiosity which emigrated has returned.
> With bright eyes it is again working
> at the side of life . . . [12]

It is there in the old and the young and in the sick and the handicapped body. It can die away, but it can also ignite every breath of air that we take with every breeze that we sense. It does not know what is coming tomorrow, but it does know that tomorrow I shall experience things that I have never experienced before. And it points beyond the death of my own body to divine creative forces which do not end with my perception and for which the word is resurrection.

9

Friendship with the Earth

However much we need a new relationship to our bodies, we also need to re-examine our ecological framework. The biblical call to human beings to exercise dominion over the earth is something which has long since been revised. 'Subdue the earth' would better describe the protective supervision of a flock by its shepherd than domination and exploitation. But so far few have thought that human beings could live in friendship with the earth. Here a children's poem about friendship is an exception: it speaks of tree, stream and wind as our friends:

> A tree can also be your friend.
> It does not speak to you, but you know
> that it likes you because it gives you apples
> or pears or cherries
> or even a branch to swing on.
>
> A stream can also be your friend,
> a quite special one.
> When it gurgles and chatters,
> it is speaking to you.
> It cools your toes,
> it lets you stand quietly on its bank
> when you don't want to talk.
>
> The wind can also be your friend.
> It sings gentle songs to you in the night
> when you are tired and alone.

Sometimes it calls you to play.
It pushes you on
and makes the leaves dance for you.
It is always around you
wherever you go,
and so you know
that it likes you.[1]

It's the same when Carter Heyward or Rubem Alves speak of 'friendship with animals and plants', an ecological movement calls itself Friends of the Earth,[2] or a verse of a women's hymn runs, 'God, friend of men and women, friend of the earth'.[3]

But today people are less interested in such friendship in nature than in the development of a caring, paternal-maternal vocabulary to signal a new way of dealing with nature, with the earth. Here theological words with a rich tradition are used, like reconciliation with nature (by the German Protestant Church), the liberation of nature (as in liberation theology), the protection and healing of creation (the Evangelical Declaration), or granting nature its rights (Reformed World Alliance). Documents talk about the preservation of creation (conciliar process) and the 'renewal' of the face of the earth – without thinking that such concepts, however well meant, can also indicate that this healing, reconciliation and preservation can also be hidden domination. The object of such concern seems to be decimated, weak, in need of help; it arouses feelings of compassion and guilt and its dignity and independence are no longer seen.

As Mary Hunt has rightly pointed out,[4] the usual epithet 'mother', as in mother earth, mother nature, has also led people astray into thinking that the mother has done her task of giving birth, has now grown old and at times is dying, where the problem with her is the problem of life. Rudolf zur Lippe is equally critical of this epithet 'mother', which communicates something of a 'snuggling up' in which one drops all claims.[5]

If, by contrast, we speak of the earth as a friend, then the mutuality of this relationship from which liveliness and responsibility for the present comes is made evident. Mother-images can lead us astray. Images of friendship present new challenges.

This independence of the earth is becoming visible again from various sources: from modern science, from the Bible and from accounts of personal experience. If we read these sources together we get an unusual, fascinating picture of the foundation on which and by which we live.[6]

I see four independent and autonomous capacities of our friend earth in dealing with people.

The creative earth

Already in the first account of creation earth the 'subjected' earth, a notion which was later to have such a fatal interpretation, is also seen as an agent. Granted, God is seen as the initiator of the event of creation in that he speaks, but at the same time the earth is also assigned an independent function.

> And God said, 'Let the earth put forth vegetation, plants yielding seed, and fruit trees bearing fruit in which is their seed, each according to its kind, upon the earth.' And it was so. The earth brought forth vegetation, plants yielding seed according to their own kinds . . . (Genesis 1.11f.).

The author of the Gospel of Mark also concedes the earth the same autonomy. He makes Jesus say:

> The kingdom of God is as if a man should scatter seed upon the ground, and should sleep and rise night and day, and the seed should sprout and grow, he knows not how. The earth produces of itself, first the blade, then the ear, then the full grain in the ear . . . (Mark 4.26f.)

In both cases the impetus comes from outside: the word of God, the sower's seed, but the emphasis and the wonderment in this process is focussed on the earth and its various processes of allowing growth. It is the mistress of the plants. Just as the earth is meant to bring forth (*blastano*), so too does the seed. The author of the Gospel of Mark has used the same (Greek) word as the creation story. Both texts are probably deliberately related. The recollection of the earth as *mater terra – magna mater* – has been preserved in Jewish-Christian creation faith. The image well-known from cosmogonies of the earth bearing the animals, as 'mistress of the animals', was also able to find a place in this account of creation:

> And God said, 'Let the earth bring forth living creatures, according to their kinds: cattle and creeping things and beasts of the earth according to their kinds. And it was so' (Genesis 1.24).

According to the Gaia hypothesis developed by the scientist J.E.Lovelock, the earth with its atmosphere and its biosphere, the constant influx of solar energy, the regular changes in temperature and so on, is a total living organism, an open system of life which takes in energy and regulates itself. A subjectivity of a distinctive kind has to be attributed to it.[7]

The earth interceding for justice

In an old text which describes Cain's murder of Abel, the earth is even depicted as an independent force creating justice:

> Then the Lord said to Cain, 'Where is Abel your brother?' He said, 'I do not know. Am I my brother's keeper?' And the Lord said, 'What have you done? The voice of your brother's blood is crying to me from the ground. And now you are cursed from the ground, which has opened its mouth to receive your brother's blood from your hand. When you till the ground, it shall no longer yield to you its strength; you shall be a fugitive and a wanderer on the earth' (Gen.4.9–12).

So the earth swallows up the blood which has been unjustly shed and refuses the perpetrator rest, fertility and success.

This idea is taken up again in the New Testament. In a discourse against scribes and Pharisees, Jesus is said to have said:

> that upon you may come all the righteous blood shed on earth, from the blood of innocent Abel to the blood of Zechariah the son of Barachiah, whom you murdered between the sanctuary and the altar (Matthew 23.35).

I see a link between blood and earth in the Gethsemane scene as narrated in Luke. According to this Jesus wrestled with death, prayed earnestly and 'his sweat became like drops of blood falling on the earth' (Luke 22.44).

The earth is polluted with the injustice of the solitude and persecution of Jesus. During his dying hours the land is visited with darkness. As in the archaic Old Testament text, so here too the earth accuses. Its pain is injustice, and it raises its own voice.

In Isaiah's expectation of the end it is said that the earth will give up the dead (26.19) and that it discloses again 'the blood which it drank', and 'no longer conceals the murdered in itself' (Isa.26.21). More than a thousand years later, Hildegard of Bingen warns against the consequence of human stupidity towards the earth:

> But the mighty voice . . . points to the lament which the elements are making to their Creator with a wild cry. You do not hear it speak in a human way, but with all the signs of its manifest subjection . . . As often as the elements of the world are hurt by the evil deeds of mankind, God will cleanse them again by human torment and tribulation.[8]

And 700 years later Dostoievsky makes Sonya say to the murderer Raskolnikov: 'Kiss the earth, because you have sinned before it.'[9]

But is such satisfaction enough? A theologian who is a geologist is now warning that the 'signs of a response in the form of massive retribution' are increasing. Now already it seems to many people that the earth is not passive and dumb. It is alive and protests. 'The earth is not dead,' declared the Korean theologian Chung Hyung Kyung at the General Assembly of the World Council of Churches in Canberra in 1991. 'It is alive and full of creative energy. The earth is a place inspired and permeated by God. For a long time human beings have exploited and raped the earth; now nature and the earth are beginning to take their revenge on us. They are refusing us clean water, clean air and other nourishment because we have sinned so gravely against it.'[10]

The earth does not allow itself to be dominated, and it does not just let things happen to it. Just as according to an old understanding it drank the blood of sacrifices and with it preserved the memory of violence and evil, so too it does not forget the violence that human beings have done to it down to the present day. It is vulnerable, but it too can wound. An old reverence and a new fear which could teach us to respect it again today unite in a humble recognition of its independence.

The helping earth

Closely connected with the notion of the just and judging earth is the aspect of its power to swallow up. Not only does it drink the blood of victims, full of compassion, and recall acts of violence. It also swallows up the evil. It is not just receptive, complaining, suffering and finally retributive. It is also a highly active authority for earthly justice. Here too it is again a partner of God. In Moses' song of praise about the annihilation of the Egyptians in the Reed Sea we read, 'You stretched out your hand and the earth swallowed them up' (Exodus 15.12). There is also a dramatic account of the rebellious group around Korah, in which the earth opened her mouth and swallowed them up (Numbers 16.28ff.).

The earth cleanses itself, and in so doing it swallows up not only the evildoers but also the evil which threatens life. In a unique biblical scene which is described in the Apocalypse, the earth drinks the river of water from a dragon which threatens to drown the pregnant woman:

> And when the dragon saw that he had been thrown down to the earth, he pursued the woman who had borne the male child. But the woman was given the two wings of the great eagle that she might fly from the serpent into the wilderness, to the place where she is to be nourished for a time, and times, and half a time. The serpent poured forth water like a river out of his mouth after the woman, to sweep her away with the flood. But the earth came to the help of the woman, and the earth opened its mouth and swallowed the river which the dragon had poured from his mouth (Revelation 12.13–16).

So far, little attention has been paid to the positive aspect of this picture: the earth helping the apocalyptic woman by swallowing up the water. The earth, which drinks up evil as a helper and friend of human beings, could hardly assert itself alongside an image of God and Father which was growing excessively powerful. Today this sisterhood of the earth and the mutuality with which we must deal with the elements is being rediscovered.

A feminist theologian describes how she interprets the scene in the Apocalypse with the earth, the woman and the dragon:

> In the wonder of the cosmic earth there is yet another source than that which is named 'God'. The earth comes to her help. Without violence it opens its mouth and swallows the water that the dragon has spewed from its jaws. Here is another unique image in the biblical tradition. It is difficult here not to imagine the old *terra mater*, the earth which soaks up the water and saves her cosmic sister. We should also note the metaphors of opening: earth-womb-dragon/spew-suck up-swallow.

This image comforts and encourages me more than that of messianic-military victory. In this book of the Bible, which anticipates the ecological damage of our century, the earth is still there for us. In itself it has the energy to save life. Today we know only too well that the earth needs our help. For me this image indicates a mutual relationship on which any authentic responsibility is orientated. But such ecological mutuality hardly has a good standing in Christian eschatology, which as a vision of transcendence constantly moves away from the earth, forwards and upwards . . .

Over and above this, a relationship to the earth means respect for and contentment with our natural body. And it means a lasting awareness of the networks which bind us to one another as earthly beings.[11]

The transforming power of the earth

A further mystery of the earth, alongside its fertility and role as an authority for justice, is its transforming power. It represents death and life, dying and becoming new. Attention to it can produce a liberating experience of transformation. This aspect becomes especially evident in the New Testament, whose texts constantly focus on the interpretation and appropriation of the message of the resurrection.

In the Gospel of Mark, which with the parable of the seed growing by itself (see p. 114) has emphasized the independent activity of the earth, two examples of the transforming power of the earth are striking. In the story of the healing of the epileptic boy there is an apparently inconspicuous sentence, 'He fell on the earth . . . ' (Mark 9.20).

This sentence no longer appears in the later Synoptic parallels. It is spoken in the middle of the healing progress, when the boy has been brought, the illness described and help asked for. After that the boy rolls around again, foam comes from his mouth, the demon is once again in full control. But for the first

time in the narrative here the body is spoken of as a subject. Up
to that point he was an object who was carried and was spoken
about.[12]

We meet the same expression, 'he fell on the earth', once
more in Mark's account of Gethsemane. This time it is Jesus,
fearful of death and being forsaken, who is said to fall on the
earth in such a way.

What is meant by this falling on the earth? In both stories,
first of all it means weakness and fear, but then also dying. It is
said of the boy that soon afterwards he lies there as if dead. A
little later Jesus dies on the cross. We also find often in the New
Testament the phrase that the grain of corn falls and dies in or
on the earth. This choice of the same word makes one think.
The ground, the earth, is the place of death, but is not the
ground/earth at the same time seen as life-giving power?

If the grain of corn dies, it brings forth much fruit (John
12.24). The boy who falls on the earth is later grasped by Jesus'
hand (the word *egeirein* – raise up, the old resurrection terminology, is used here!) and he then stands up by himself (he has
risen!). The same fate is narrated of Jesus. It seems to me that in
all three cases the contact with the earth denotes contact with
death, nearness to death, which at the same time represents the
presupposition for new life, fertility and resurrection. The earth
with its mysterious power brings about both dying and becoming new, death and life. In the New Testament the image of this
ambiguous earth is often an image of new life. So new life is life
which renews itself, not an absolute new creation.

The same experiences of earth appear in two biographies
from recent decades. When she is told of the death of her husband, Clara von Arnim experiences this life-giving power of
dying and rising:

It was a beautiful sunny day. The children were playing outside. I went into the wood near by. I threw myself down on
the brown, dry ground among the spruce trees, for here in the

wood I could weep. I wept for a long time, perhaps an hour. Then I got up.[13]

The Jewish girl Janina David describes even more impressively the way in which she experienced the news of the death of her parents:

> I turned over and hid my face in the long grass. The earth revolved with terrifying speed, rushed through the eternal night, and I clung on with both hands, pressed myself to its unyielding service. If only I could be under it too, like all those who were already peacefully dead and buried! How safe I would finally feel. But I was outside, the earth did not yet want me, and there was no way to those who were already under it. It made no sense to strike it with my fists and beg it to let me in. I had to live out the time allotted to me to the end – alone.
>
> I closed my eyes, pressed my back against the earth and repeated loudly: 'My parents are dead. They died in a concentration camp or, betrayed by their fellow citizens, on a street in the city. I shall never know how, when or precisely where that happened and where they are buried. There will be no grave to receive their mortal remains. This whole land is a grave, the whole earth is a giant grave, and somewhere they are part of it. Now I can go on, but as long as I can touch the earth, I am also bound up with them.'
>
> The radiant heaven shone through my half-closed eyes. A shining pattern of leaves danced against its hard blue background. I awoke after a long sleep in which the smell of apples and pears ripening in the sun had returned by a miracle and even now still filled the air around me. The earth was soft, I lay on my back, felt the ground yield under me like a warm cradle. Grass grew between my fingers and over my body; ants crawled over my legs. I looked at them calmly, without a shiver of fear. They and I, we all belonged to the earth. It was the only indestructible foundation of our

existence. It gave us life, and one day we shall all return to it. That was the only certainty, the only comfort. From the orchards dreaming in the autumn sun the wind brought the scent of ripening fruit. The scent of returning life. The scent of peace.[14]

At the end of their lives human beings – themselves a bit of earth (*adama*) – will return to this earth.

Knowledge of our bond with the earth in creation always has two aspects: mourning and comfort. Mourning for the decay of the body, which decays like the earth, and comfort because this body, with this earth, returns to the alliance of creation. There is something of such a hope in our funeral liturgy: 'From the earth you were taken and to the earth you will return. From this earth Jesus Christ will awaken you at the Last Day.'

We have a document with a similar thought from the seventh century. The epitaph for Gregory the Great reads, '*Suscipe Terra tuo de corpore sumptum*' (Receive, O earth, what was taken from your body) – a perhaps last Christian remembrance that mother earth was still alive under Christians and did not threaten Christian belief in God.[15]

What can such old stories about the earth say to men and women today?

Seeing the earth as independent limits our fantasies of omnipotence, allows us again to learn wonderment and reverence, and to see ourselves in an alliance with creation and all creatures. Knowing this archaic power of the earth, men and women can then also become friends of the earth and help it to regenerate itself. In this knowledge they have to protect and preserve it from human stupidity and greed, but they can do that only if they remember their own dignity and a sacred materiality which God offers us with it. We must learn once again to experience this holiness of the earth, our body and everyday things around us. Friendship is a way to shape our lives in this power of the earth.

Closing Thoughts

Women have begun to rediscover the secret power of the earth that lies in friendship between women. But not only for themselves. The earthings that they describe, the way that friendship specifically comes into being in touching, in hearing, in celebrations and in everyday life, in their discovery of their own personalities and in the dignity of the earth, in the magic of mutuality, cannot leave untouched the world in which they live. It is no longer a matter of being 'a friend's friend', as Schiller's 'Ode to Joy' has it, and at the same time attaining a 'glorious woman'. More is offered us with friendship. An everyday experience like friendship can break open the alienations and hostilities with which we arm ourselves. An everyday word like friendship can break down the hierarchies which cement our orders and melt the blocks of ice which have built up between God and us.

Often we do not see friends, and experience no friendship. There is a children's poem which is called 'A friend is someone who loves you'. It says, 'If you think you have no friends, you must stop and think whether someone hasn't perhaps smiled at you in his own way', then we can smile back and discover what is done to us and what does us good.

Friendships can entail effort and work. They are not always easy. But what then opens up under the blockages of alienation and mistrust or merely indifference changes us and our view of the world. Curiosity makes us bold and enthusiastic. The cup of tea at the kitchen table again allows everyday food to be tasted as divine energy. The earth which gives us calm and relaxation again becomes holy. The independence of our bodies can become a miracle. The 'other' becomes attractive.

That God has become human opens up for us in ever new dimensions as a miracle in which we take part with hands, hearts and senses.

Everything that we take for granted, the divisions that we suffer, the artificial separations that we maintain – friendship can change all this. To live in friendship is a process which makes us friendly and attentive, tender and precise, and in which we wake up to experience something of the diversity of the secret power of God's earth.

Women, my friends, wake up!

Notes

Introduction

1. Virginia Woolf, *A Room of One's Own* (1929), Penguin Books 1993, 74, 79.
2. See S. Eickenrodt and C. Rapisarda, *Querelles, Jahrbuch für Frauenforschung 1998. Freundschaft im Gespräch*, Stuttgart and Weimar 1998, 17ff., for what follows. For friendships between women in the history of Christianity see Monika Barz, Herta Leistner and Ute Wild, *Hättest du gedacht, dass wir so viele sind? Lesbische Fragen in der Kirche*, Stuttgart 1987, 139ff.
3. Ibid., 157.
4. Hans van der Gees, *Unter vier Augen. Beispiele gelungener Seelsorge*, Zurich 1986, 235.
5. Kurt Marti, *Zärtlichkeit und Schmerz*, Neuwied 1979, 66.
6. Dagmar Schultz (ed.), *Macht und Sinnlichkeit*, Berlin 1983.
7. Klaus-Peter Jörns, *Die neuen Gesichter Gottes*, Munich 1997.
8. See Heinrich Meyer, *Die Lehre Carl Schmitts*, Stuttgart 1994, 109ff.
9. Anne Wilson Schaef, *Weibliche Wirklichkeit*, Wildberg 1985, 161ff.
10. Sallie McFague, *Models of God*, Philadelphia and London 1988, 173.
11. An impressive book on friendship is John O'Donohue, *Anam Cara*, Munich 1997, which describes Celtic wisdom based on the monastic tradition of 'soul friend'. A collection of sketches of religious friendships which has appeared in the USA, L.S. Rouner, *The Changing Face of Friendship*, Notre Dame 1994, does not get beyond an androcentric contribution (with the exception of Mary Hunt's account). Walter Sparn, 'Und schweigend umarmt ihn der treue Freund', *Reformatio* 48, 1999, 136ff., makes a profound contribution on the absence of friendship from theology.

1. Traditions of Friendship with God

1. Thus Erik Peterson, *Der Gottesfreund*, 2 KG XL, II.Band, Neue Folge V, 1923, 161–202. For a comprehensive treatment of friendship in cultural history see Igor S. Kon, *Freundschaft*, Reinbek 1979. John F. Fitzgerald (ed.), *Greco-Roman Perspectives on Friendship*, Atlanta 1997, investigates friendship in the Graeco-Roman and New Testament contexts.
2. Sallie McFague, *Models of God*, London and Philadelphia 1988, 173.
3. Rudolf Butmann, *The Gospel of John*, Oxford and Philadelphia 1971, 544.
4. Adolf von Harnack, *Mission und Ausbreitung des Christentums* I, Leipzig 1906, 353f.
5. See Margot Schmidt, 'Theologin', in *Wörterbuch der Feministischen Theologie*, ed. E. Gössmann et al., Gütersloh 1991, 402, on Mechthild of Hackeborn. Hanna-Barbara Gerl also sees Hildegard of Bingen's theology as being stamped with 'friendship' and God as the 'primal friend'. Unfortunately, however, as far as I can see, the terms 'friend' and 'friendship' do not appear in these contexts (H.B. Gerl, *Freundinnen*, Munich 1993, 37ff.).
6. Meister Eckhart, *Ewige Geburt*, Gütersloh 1948, 171.
7. Waltraud Herbstrith, *Aufbruch nach innen*, Munich 1998, 105.
8. *Die Legenda aurea des Jacobus de Voragine*, Heidelberg 1979, 472.
9. Gerta Scharffenorth, *Den Glauben ins Leben ziehen*. Munich 1982, 158f.; ead., *Freunde in Christus werden . . .*, Gelnhausen 1977.
10. Dorle Schönhals-Schlaudt, 'Du Eva, komm sing dein Lied', in *Frauen fordern eine gerechte Sprache*, Gütersloh 1990, 136.

2. From Friendship with God to Friendship between Women

1. Jürgen Moltmann, *Church in the Power of the Spirit*, London and New York 1977; *The Open Church*, London and Philadelphja 1978.
2. Sallie McFague, *Metaphorical Theology*, Philadelphia and London 1982; *Models of God*, Philadelphia and London 1987; *The Body of God*, Minneapolis and London 1993.
3. Ead., *Metaphorical Theology* (n.2), 190. Also in her later books, *Models of God* and *The Body of God*, she avoids fixing herself on feminist theology. In a Würzburg diploma thesis Hildegard Wustman has interpreted Sallie McFague's later book *Models of God* in feminist terms and read the metaphor of woman friend out of McFague's 'friend' (*Wenn Gott zur Freundin wird*, Frankfurt 1993). But as far as I can see, McFague deliberately maintains the neutral 'friend'.
4. Carter Heyward, *The Redemption of God*, New York 1982.
5. Mary Hunt, *Fierce Tenderness. A Feminist Theology of Friendship*,

New York 1991.

6. Ibid., 10, 150.
7. Hildegund Keul, *Menschenwerden durch Berühren. Bettina Brentano-Arnim als Wegbereiterin für eine Feministische Theologie*, Frankfurt 1993.
8. Ibid., 154.
9. Ibid., 339.

3. *Jesus, the Friend*

1. Frauenarbeit der Evangelische Landesskirche in Württemberg (ed.), *Wir Frauen und das Herrenmahl*, 1996. See also what follows. For criticism of atoning sacrifice see e.g. Hans Kessler, *Die theologische Bedeutung des Todes Jesu*, Düsseldorf 1970.
2. Elisabeth Schüssler Fiorenza, *Jesus – Miriam's Child, Sophia's Prophet*, New York and London 1995, 113.
3. Mary Hunt, *Fierce Tenderness. A Feminist Theology of Friendship*, New York 1991, 10, 150.
4. Ibid., 19.
5. Elisabeth Schüssler Fiorenza, *In Memory of Her*, New York and Lonon ²1995, 127ff.
6. Ibid., 119f.
7. See *Wir Frauen und das Herrenmahl* (n.1), 32. Here there is also an illustration of the large-scale depiction of a women's eucharist by the artist Candace Carter.
8. Felix Christ, *Jesus Sophia*, Zurich 1970, 154.
9. See Elisabeth Moltmann-Wendel, *A Land Flowing with Milk and Honey*, London and New York 1986. For Christa Mulack, *Jesus – der Gesalbte der Frauen*, Stuttgart 1987, Jesus even becomes the anointed of women.
10. Rita Nakashima Brock, *Journeys by Heart*, New York 1988, 98.
11. See Helga Kuhlmann, 'Solus Christus?', in Jost and Valtink, *Ihr aber, für wen haltet ihr mich?*, Gütersloh 1996, 50ff.
12. Doris Strahm, *Vom Rand in die Mitte*, Lucerne 1997, 236.
13. Ibid., 262. See Delores Williams, *Sisters in the Wilderness*, New York 1993, 202: Jesus as 'helpmate'.
14. Ibid., 240.
15. Ute Gerhard et al., *Dem Reich der Freiheit werb' ich Bürgerinnen*, Frankfurt 1980, 106. Here Otto-Peters refers to Jesus' friendship with Mary and Martha.
16. See Schüssler Fiorenza, *In Memory of Her* (n.5), 147.

4. The Last Supper as a Meal of Friendship

1. See Frauenarbeit der Evangelische Landesskirche in Württemberg (ed.), *Wir Frauen und das Herrenmahl*, 1996; Ute Grümbel, *Abendmahl, Für Euch gegeben*, Stuttgart 1997.
2. René Girard, *Das Ende der Gewalt*, Freiburg 1983, 212. ET *Violence and the Sacred*, London 1977.
3. Ibid, 187. Grümbel's survey of women and men about their understanding of the eucharist indicates clearly that women express scepticism about the significance of sacrifice and victims (251). Only three of twenty-eight women questioned spoke along the lines of the traditional interpretation of the death of Jesus in terms of atonement (253).
4. Hans Kessler, 'Das Kreuz und die Auferstehung', in H. Schmidinger (ed.), *Jesus von Nazareth*, Graz 1995, 165. Unfortunately the German language does not distinguish between victim and sacrifice, as English does.
5. Eduard Schweizer, *Good News according to Mark*, London 1966, ad loc.
6. Ahn Byung-Mu, 'Jesus und Minjung im Markusevangelium', in *Minjung. Theologie des Volkes Gottes in Südkorea*, ed. J. Moltmann, 1984, 113ff.
7. Ibid., 120.
8. In her survey Grümbel established a far greater interest among women in a shared meal; sensual, bodily experience is significant only for a few men (331).
9. Jutta Anna Kleber, 'Zucht und Ekstase', in A. Schuller and J. Kleber, *Verschlemmte Welt*, Göttingen 1994, 235ff.
10. Ibid., 249.
11. K. Marti, *Zärtlichkeit und Schmerz*, Neuwied 1979, 131.

5. Separation from God and Goodness

1. Luise Rinser, *Den Wolf umarmen*, Frankfurt 1981, 101.
2. V.S. Goldstein, 'Die menschliche Situation: ein weiblicher Standpunkt', in E. Moltmann-Wendel, *Menschenrechte für die Frau*, Munich 1974, 123.
3. However, feminist theologians have similarly preserved statements about the fundamental corruption of humankind, above all in relation to sexist structures. See Lucia Scherzberg, *Sünde und Gnade in der Feministischen Theologie*, Mainz 1991, 60, 116f.
4. Christina Thürmer-Rohr, *Vagabundinnen*, Berlin 1987, 49ff.
5. Christa Mulack, . . . *und wieder fühle ich mich schuldig*, Stuttgart 1993.

6. Christine Schaumberger and Luise Schottroff, *Schuld und Macht*, Munich 1988, 275ff.

7. Valerie C.Saiving, 'Our Bodies/Our Selves', *Journal of Feminist Studies in Religion*, 1988, Vol.4. no.2, 117ff.

8. Erich Fromm, *Haben oder sein*, Stuttgart 1967, 357ff.

9. Thus Marjorie Hewitt Suchocki, 'Sünde: Rebellion gegen die Schöpfung', in Brand, Suchocki, Welker, *Sünde*, Neukirchen 1997, 35ff.

10. Matthew Fox, *Original Blessing*, Santa Fé 1983, 54ff.

6. *Jesus' Friend – Mary Magdalene*

1. From the extensive literature on Mary Magdalene I can mention only a few titles here: Dietmar Bader (ed.), *Maria Magdalena – Zu einem Bild der Frau in der christlichen Verkündigung*, Freiburg 1990; Elisabeth Moltmann-Wendel, *The Women around Jesus*, London and New York 1982; ead., 'Frauen und Männer am Wege Jesu', in H.Schmidinger (ed.), *Jesus von Nazareth*, Graz 1995; Carla Ricci, *Mary Magdalene and Many Others*, Minneapolis 1994.

2. See Moltmann-Wendel, *The Women around Jesus* (n.1), 61ff.

3. Karl Künstle, *Ikonographie der christlichen Kunst*, Freibuirg 1926. There is a splendid account of the Augustinian fear of sin and sex in Elaine Pagels, *Adam, Eve and the Serpent*, London and New York 1989.

4. Hennecke-Schneelmelcher-Wilson, *New Testament Apocrypha* I, Louisville and Cambridge ²1991, 194, 394.

5. *Die Legenda aurea des Jacobus de Voragine*, Heidelberg 1979, 472.

6. Ernst Eggimann, *Jesus-Texte* © 'Peter Schifferli Verlags AG, Die Arche, Zurich.

7. Heinrich Böll in an interview, *Internationale Dialogzeitschrift* 69/4.

8. Thus the German Mary Magdalene Society's initiative for equal rights for women in the church, at its tenth anniversary in Münster in 1997.

9. Libreria delle donne di Milano, *Wie weiblich Freiheit ensteht*, ³1991.

10. Gottfried Koch, *Frauenfrage und Ketzertum im Mittelalter*, Berlin 1962, 100.

11. Shulamith Shahar, *Die Frau im Mittelalter*, Frankfurt 1983, 105.

12. Christina Thürmer-Rohr, 'Denken der Differenz. Feminismus und Postmoderne', in *Utopie. Richtiges im Falschen* 18, 1995, 94ff.

13. David Tracy, 'Fragments and Forms. University and Particularity Today', in Giuseppi Ruggieri and Miklós Tomka (eds), *The Church in Fragments: Towards What Kind of Unity?*, *Concilium* 1997/3, 125.

7. *Friendly Contacts: Tenderness and Eros*

1. S.B. and L. Wachinger, 'Zärtlichkeit', in Lissner et al. (eds), *Frauen-lexikon*, 1185.
2. Erich Fromm, *Die Kunst des Liebens*, Frankfurt 1980, 66.
3. Heinrich Böll in an interview, *Internationale Dialogzeitschrift* 69/4.
4. Id., 'Versuch über die Vernunft der Poesie', *Frankfurter Allgemeine Zeitung*, 3 May 1973.
5. *Unsere Hoffnung, Ein Beschluss der Gemeinsamen Synode der Bistümer i.d.BRS Deutschland.*
6. Kurt Marti, *Zärtlichkeit und Schmerz*, Darmstadt 1979, 66.
7. Ibid., 68.
8. Wolfgang Dietrich, *GegenSätze. Antithesen im Sinne Jesu*, Eschbach, nd, 48.
9. Dagmar Schultz (ed.), *Macht und Sinnlichkeit*, Berlin 1983, 160.
10. Dietmar Mieth, *Die Kunst, zärtlich zu sein*, Freiburg 1987.
11. Christina Thürmer-Rohr, 'Lust – Verlust der Frau – ein Wundmal', in A. Deuber-Mankowski et al., *Die Revolution hat nicht stattgefunden*, Tübingen 1989, 303ff.
12. Evelyn Fox Keller, *Liebe, Macht und Erkenntnis*, Munich 1986.
13. Rita Nakashima Brock, *Journeys by Heart*, New York 1988.
14. Anders Nygren, *Agape and Eros*, London 1932-39 (3 vols).
15. Dietmar Mieth, 'Liebe', in Lissner et al. (eds), *Frauenlexikon*, 648.
16. Christos Yannaras, *Person und Eros*, Göttingen 1982, 122ff.
17. Annie Berner-Hürbin, *Eros die subtile Energie*, Basel 1989, 16f., 172, 210f.
18. Ina Praetorius, *Skizzen zur feministischen Ethik*, Mainz 1995, 47ff.

8. *My Body – My Friend*

1. Rubem Alves, *I Believe in the Resurrection of the Body*, Maryknoll, NY 1980.
2. Starhawk, 'Witchcraft as Goddess Religion', in C.Spretnak, *The Politics of Women's Spirituality*, New York 1982, 51.
3. Ingrid Olbricht, *Die Brust*, Reinbek 1989; ead., *Alles psychisch?*, Munich 1989, 265; ead., *Was Frauen krank macht*, Munich 1993, 243, 265.
4. Barbara Duden, 'Entkörperung im Dienst der Gesundheitsthesen zur Veränderung der Selbstwahrnehmung von Frauen . . . ', in *Von der 'Krankheit' Frau zur Fraugesundheit. Dokumentation der 4. Jahres-tagung des AKF*, 1997.
5. Christa Wolf, preface to Maxie Wander, *Guten Morgen, Du Schöne*, Darmstadt 1978, 15. Carola Meier-Seethaler, *Gefühl und Urteils-*

kraft, Munich 1998, is a passionate plea for feeling, embodiment and emotional reason.

6. epd-Dokumentation, *Welche Natur wollen wir? Welche Natur haben wir?*, 17/91, 71.

7. Beverley Wildung Harrison, 'Die Macht des Zorns im Werk der Liebe', in Brooten and Greinacher, *Frauen in der Männenkirche*, Munich 1982, 199f.

8. Anne Wilson Schaef, *Weibliche Wirklichkeit*, Wildberg 1985, 154.

9. Ina Praetorius, *Skizzen zur feministischen Ethik*, Mainz 1995, 50ff.

10. Nelle Morton, 'Auf dem Weg zu einer ganzheitlicher Theologie', in E. Moltmann-Wendel, *Frau und Religion*, Frankfurt 1983, 202ff. For what follows see E. Moltmann-Wendel, *I am my Body*, London 1994.

11. Hannah Arendt, *Vita activa*, Munich 1960, 243, etc.; Annegret Stopczyk, *Nein danke, ich denke selber*, Berlin 1996, 195f.

12. Marie-Luise Kaschnitz, *Dein Schweigen – meine Stimme*, Munich 1962, 107.

9. *Friendship with the Earth*

1. Joan Walsh Anglund, *Ein Freund is jemand, der dich gern hat*, Olten 1958.

2. Mary Hunt, *Fierce Tenderness. A Feminist Theology of Friendship*, New York 1991, 173. The German BUND emerged from this.

3. Dorle Schönhals-Schlaudt, *Du Eva, komm sing dein Lied*, 1993, 9.

4. Hunt, *Fierce Tenderness* (n.2), 173.

5. Rudolf zur Lippe, 'Natur und Ästhetik', in epd Dokumentation, *Welche Natur wollen wir? Welche Natur haben wir?*, 17/91.

6. For more detail see E. Moltmann, M. Schwelien, B. Stamer, *Erde, Quelle, Baum, Lebenssymbole in Märchen, Bibel und Kunst*, Stuttgart 1994.

7. J.E. Lovelock, *Gaia – A New Look at Life on Earth*, London 1979; D. Sagan and L. Margulis, 'Gaia and Philosophy', in L.S. Rouner (ed.), *On Nature*, Boston University Studies in Philosophy and Religion, Notre Dame 1974, 60–78.

8. *Illuminations of Hildegard of Bingen*, Commentary by Matthew Fox, Santa Fé 1985, II.

9. F.M. Dostoievsky, *Crime and Punishment*, Harmondsworth 1997.

10. Chung Hyung Kyung, 'Komm, Heiliger Geist – erneuere die ganze Schöpfung', *Junge Kirche* 3/91, 130ff. See also ead., *Struggle to Be the Sun Again*, Maryknoll, NY and London 1991.

11. Catherine Keller, 'Die Frau in der Wüste. Ein feministisch-theologischer Midrasch zu Apk 12', *Evangelische Theologie* 5/90, 414ff.

12. The complete text is in Konrad von Bonin (ed.), *Deutscher Evangelischer Kirchentag Ruhrgebiet* 1991, Munich 1991, 74ff.
13. Clara von Arnim, *Der grüne Baum des Lebens*, Munich 1989, 363.
14. Janina David, *Ein Stück Erde*, Knaur Taschenbuch, 204.
15. *The Woman's Encyclopedia of Myths and Secrets*, San Francisco 1983, 264.